SCHOLARS

OF

MAYHEM

SCHOLARS

OF

MAYHEM

MY FATHER'S SECRET WAR
IN NAZI-OCCUPIED FRANCE

DANIEL C. GUIET AND TIMOTHY K. SMITH

PENGUIN PRESS

New York

PENGUIN PRESS
An imprint of Penguin Random House LLC
penguinrandomhouse.com

Library of Congress Cataloging-in-Publication Data
Names: Guiet, Daniel (Daniel C.), author. | Smith, Timothy (Timothy K.), author.
Title: Scholars of mayhem : my father's secret war in Nazi-occupied France /
Daniel C. Guiet and Timothy K. Smith.
Description: New York : Penguin Press, 2019. | Includes bibliographical references and index.
Identifiers: LCCN 2018060307 (print) | LCCN 2019000575 (ebook) |
ISBN 9780735225213 (ebook) | ISBN 9780735225206 (hardcover)
Subjects: LCSH: Guiet, Jean Claude. | Spies--United States--Biography. |
Espionage, American--France--History--20th century. | Great Britain. Special Operations
Executive--Biography. | World War, 1939-1945--Secret service--Great Britain. |
World War, 1939-1945--Military intelligence--France. | World War,
1939-1945--Underground movements--France. | Espionage, British--France.
Classification: LCC D810.S8 (ebook) | LCC D810.S8 G83 2019 (print) |
DDC 940.54/2142092 [B] --dc23
LC record available at https://lccn.loc.gov/2018060307

Map on pp. ix illustrated by Daniel Lagin

Printed in the United States of America
1   3   5   7   9   10   8   6   4   2

Pp. x, 4, 5, 55, 79, 80, 126, 150, 155, 158, 198, 206, 218: Jean Claude Guiet's collection of OSS
and SOE memorabilia, digitized and held by the International Museum of World War II in Natick,
MA; *pp. 20, 214:* Imperial War Museum; *p. 112:* Museum of Tulle Collection, Funds MRD, 1PH
1953, reproduction of the drawing of the hangings of Tulle June 9, 1944 (anonymous author). With
thanks to the Pôle Musées de la Ville de Tulle; *pp. 184–187:* Letter by Wing Commander Forest
Yeo-Thomas, Crown copyright 1944; *p. 209:* Photograph by Carol Guiet; *p. 218:* Certified Chinese
translation provided by Samuel Chong of Abacus Consulting Services, Alhambra, CA 91801; *p. 234:*
Jean Claude Guiet's collection of OSS and SOE memorabilia, photographed by Scott DW Smith.

DESIGNED BY NICOLE LAROCHE

CONTENTS

══ PART THREE ══

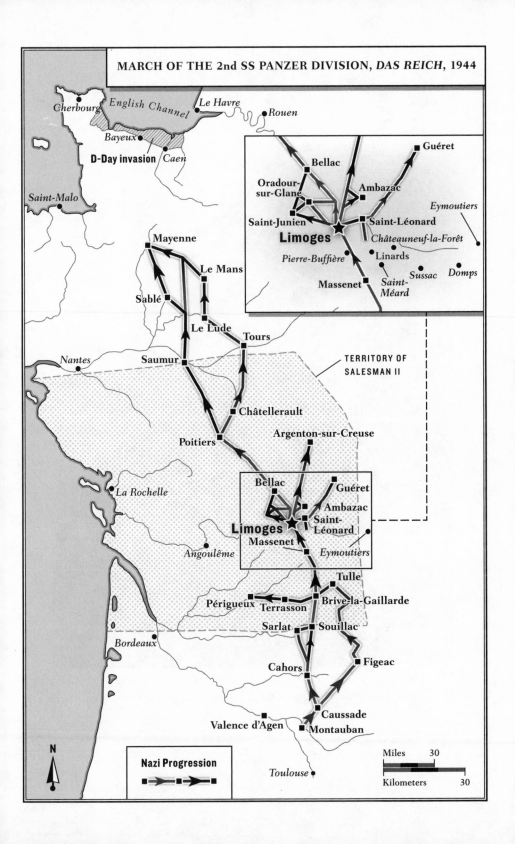

MARCH OF THE 2nd SS PANZER DIVISION, *DAS REICH*, 1944

English Channel

Cherbourg

Le Havre

Rouen

Bayeux

Caen

D-Day invasion

Saint-Malo

Bellac

Oradour-sur-Glane

Ambazac

Guéret

Eymoutiers

Saint-Junien

Saint-Léonard

Limoges

Châteauneuf-la-Forêt

Pierre-Buffière

Linards

Massenet

Saint-Méard

Sussac

Domps

Mayenne

Le Mans

Sablé

Le Lude

Tours

Nantes

Saumur

TERRITORY OF SALESMAN II

Châtellerault

Argenton-sur-Creuse

Poitiers

La Rochelle

Bellac

Guéret

Ambazac

Limoges

Saint-Léonard

Massenet

Eymoutiers

Angoulême

Tulle

Périgueux

Terrasson

Brive-la-Gaillarde

Sarlat

Souillac

Bordeaux

Cahors

Figeac

Caussade

Valence d'Agen

Montauban

Toulouse

N

Nazi Progression

Miles 30

Kilometers 30

First Lieutenant Jean Claude Guiet, age twenty, in December 1944.

FOREWORD

I stood with my father, Jean Claude Guiet, by a corrugated metal hangar at the Lons-le-Saunier airport in eastern France, watching a blue-and-white Cessna 182 make its final approach. Jean Claude did not allow the anticipation he felt to show in his expression. It was 9:00 A.M. on a sunny summer day that promised to build into a very hot Jura afternoon. A single tattered wind sock fluttered in the light breeze.

The Cessna was an old one, perfectly ordinary, except that someone had removed its transponder, the device that would have identified it to air traffic controllers. Its pilot was Bob Maloubier, a seventy-seven-year-old Frenchman wearing Ray-Bans and a handlebar mustache. In the copilot's seat rode his friend and former wife, Catherine, a beautiful and easygoing woman some twenty years his junior.

Five days before, on June 24, 2000, Bob and Jean Claude had been reunited for the first time since the liberation of Paris in 1944. They had both attended the opening of a museum in Wormelow, England, devoted to the memory of Violette Szabo, an English secret agent who was a heroine of the French Resistance. Bob, who stood six foot four, wore a chest full of medals and ribbons. Jean Claude, who was five ten, wore none of his. Their handshake turned into a long embrace.

"My God, Jean, you've gotten very old!" Bob said in French. Jean Claude replied, "I am still six months younger than you."

The museum opening was a merry hubbub of war veterans, politicians, even a few movie stars, and the newspaper reporters and BBC film crew competing to interview them. It was no place for a real conversation. So Bob and Jean Claude agreed to have a private reunion at the little château where my wife, Carol, and I spend summers in Nevy-sur-Seille, a village of 250 souls in the Jura region. Bob would fly in from Paris, where he lived. They would have a chance to go over the extraordinary history they had shared with Violette, and also news about the fifty-six years since they had seen each other last.

We watched the Cessna descend toward the grassy airstrip bordered by white-painted rocks. My father's face betrayed nothing. I was aflame with curiosity, especially as I knew that the wartime records of the unit both men had served with had finally been declassified. My father, a discreet, formal, French-born American—a perfectionist in all he did—had never spoken of things that were officially secret.

My thoughts drifted to the tin bread box that had traveled with our family everywhere the government-supplied moving vans took us during my peripatetic childhood. It was light gray, painted with pink hibiscus flowers. Wherever we lived—apartment, hotel, shanty, or house—the box would be tucked away in a hard-to-reach spot in my father's bedroom closet. There was never any food in it—it gave off no scent of crackers, bread, or nuts. Rather it smelled faintly of rubberized plastic, with undertones of old leather and canvas. We children didn't have to be told never to touch it; the box, it was understood, was strictly off-limits.

Opening it required considerable strength in the fingertips, I discovered at age five. We were living in a Quonset hut on Saipan that year, 1956. My parents and my older sister were outside on the beach, taking in a picture-perfect Pacific sunset. The tin bread box had been placed within my reach for once, on the Quonset hut's floor among crates and suitcases, as we were preparing to move yet again. I got my fingers under the narrow, rolled lip of the lid, popped it, and peered inside.

I didn't understand most of the things I found. The .45 automatic was not a mystery, to be sure; I removed it carefully, along with five full clips. There were three slim knives, about four to ten inches long, in leather sheaths with straps. There was also a length of wire with a wooden handle at each end.

There were thin pieces of paper, four inches square, titled Field Station to Home Station and Home Station to Field Station, with tiny type printed on them in sequences of five random letters. There were black-and-white photos, with scalloped white borders, of men roasting monkeys in a jungle.

I found passports and identification cards that bore my father's photograph but names that were not his. There was a compass. A small green box, bound with a fat rubber band, contained narrow bits of metal with quarter-inch round wooden handles—a set of lock rakes, as I later learned. There were large silk squares imprinted with different countries' flags, bearing messages in unfamiliar alphabets. The messages, I discovered much later, were variations on a theme: *I am an American. Take me to the nearest Allied military office. You will be paid.*

I put everything back into the box in the correct sequence and snapped the lid shut.

The Cessna kissed the runway, its wheels sinking a little way into the grass, and taxied to the hangar. Bob and Catherine climbed out of the plane and into our car. It was a short ride to the château, along the bank of the Seille River, through the village, through our gated wall, past our little vineyard and trout pond and up to the 250-year-old house. We settled on the terrace with coffee.

Bob began by asking Jean Claude, "What did you do after being dragged off to the airport by the MPs?"

He was alluding to their parting, in Paris, in September 1944. The two young men had survived their clandestine mission in occupied

France, against long odds, and had made their way to the liberated capital. For four days they celebrated their good fortune, drinking, dancing, and dining in Paris's very expensive, very good, black-market restaurants. They had no desire to report to their commanding officers just yet, and that meant eluding the military policemen who patrolled the city rounding up reveling soldiers. Jean Claude had two sets of papers, one French, one American, and he was perfectly bilingual. He was able to fool the French MPs by speaking only English when questioned, and the Americans by speaking French, but his luck ran out on day four when he was picked up by a joint French-American patrol. They took him in for questioning and ascertained his true identity. A few hours later an older man in civilian clothing arrived hurriedly and, escorted by two MPs, put Jean Claude on the next flight to London.

"I spent a few days at Baker Street," Jean Claude replied.

Number 64 Baker Street in London was, at that time, the headquarters of an organization called the Special Operations Executive (SOE). The few people who knew of its existence nicknamed it the Ministry of Ungentlemanly Warfare. Its operatives were sometimes called the Baker Street Irregulars.

For any reader unfamiliar with the Sherlock Holmes canon, the original Baker Street Irregulars were London urchins who, in several stories, did intelligence work for the great detective. The men and women of SOE were certainly irregular in many senses of the word, but it wouldn't be quite right to think of them as spies. They were secret agents, to be sure, but they weren't trained just for espionage. Their job was mayhem—sabotage and subversion behind enemy lines. As one SOE officer told the historian M. R. D. Foot:

"Our field operatives were for the most part temperamentally unable to regard Intelligence as anything but the essential prelude to action. To whet their appetites for action, by directing them to locate enemy activities or resources, and at the same time to forbid action, is akin to giving a lion a raw sirloin to play with but not to eat."[1]

The two old lions conversing at the château were the surviving members of a four-person team that parachuted into Nazi-occupied France, near Limoges, on the day after D-Day. There they galvanized thousands of *maquisards*—rural bands of French guerrillas—to intercept German reinforcements and prevent them from reaching Normandy. Bob was a demolition specialist. Jean Claude was the team's wireless operator, responsible for coded communications with Baker Street. They were not expected to survive.

Before they got into the details of their wartime mission, though, Bob and Jean Claude had some catching up to do.

Jean Claude told Bob that after his return to Baker Street he had been shipped home to Northampton, Massachusetts, where both his parents were professors at Smith College. Then it was off to California for jungle training with the Office of Strategic Services, the CIA precursor headed by William Donovan—"Wild Bill"—known as the father of American Intelligence. Jean Claude's OSS team was sent to China to train tribesmen in guerrilla warfare against Japanese and Communist Chinese troops.

Bob told Jean Claude that he too had been sent to fight in the Pacific theater.

Jean Claude said the warfare he had witnessed while living among Kachin and Naga tribesmen had been especially savage. He had seen necklaces made of ears, and the shrunken heads of Japanese soldiers.

Bob stared quietly into Jean Claude's face and said that he had seen similar things in Vietnam and Laos.

Jean Claude said that in China you could never really be sure who was friend or foe. Even the regular U.S. Army resented and distrusted the OSS men. Eventually hostilities became so great that the army filed court-martial charges against Jean Claude; Wild Bill ordered him to disappear for a month, and when he resurfaced he found the charges dropped.

Bob knew what that was like. He too had hidden out in a jungle, later in his career, when he managed to get crosswise with both the Corsican Mafia and the Mossad. He had flown the blue-and-white Cessna from France to a lumber camp in the Congo. That was how he had met Catherine, the daughter of a French foreign service couple posted to that country. They had two children, and remained close after their divorce.

As they talked, the two men switched languages from time to time—French to English and back again—occasionally testing one another with a phrase in Italian, Spanish, or German.

Jean Claude told Bob that after the atomic bombs ended the war, he went back to Massachusetts and reenrolled at Harvard. He graduated magna cum laude, obtained a master's degree in Romance languages, and attempted to follow the family teaching tradition by taking a position in the French Department at Ohio State University. His first semester there he taught four classes, and it became clear that his perfectionism was going to be a problem: He flunked every student in every class he taught. The university put him on probation. The second semester he did it again, insisting, with documentation, that each student deserved a failing grade. It was something of a relief when he was invited to join many of his old colleagues from Europe and Indochina in the newly formed Central Intelligence Agency.

Bob had returned to France at war's end with a severe case of malaria. Recovered after a few months, he helped found the *Service de Documentation Extérieure et de Contre-Espionnage* (External Documentation and Counter-Espionage Service, SDECE). For a number of years he operated a covert school for the SDECE in Austria, recruiting, training, and running agents in Russia and its satellites.

We opened a bottle of Crémant du Jura, a local sparkling wine, and strolled outside into the heat, glasses in hand. It was clear that Bob and Jean Claude were done with their summing-up: Neither man would ask for details of the other's Cold War clandestine service, or volunteer his own.

We found shade under a huge sequoia. Bob turned to Jean Claude and asked him in a curiously loud voice if he ever had difficult dreams, dark memories, or bouts of anxiety stemming from their SOE operation in the Limousin region. Bob said that sometimes he had trouble sleeping. Jean Claude said he did too, recalling his terror of being detected and captured each time he switched on his radio set.

Bob asked my father if anyone knew how many *maquisard* fighters had been killed working for their team. Jean Claude said he didn't have even a rough idea, but that it had to have been well over a couple of thousand. Their ghostly army, drawing fighters from eight departments of central France, had numbered about ten thousand at its peak. But these were citizen soldiers—farmers, teachers, shopkeepers, laborers—and their sacrifices were not recorded in any formal ledger. Records kept by SOE, scanty to begin with for security's sake, were mostly destroyed by fire during and after the war.

Jean Claude stared down at leaves and branches and said quietly that every June 10 he took some private time to honor the memory of Violette. Bob nodded in agreement and pretended to search the horizon. This was their first opportunity to talk about these things, openly and legally, in more than half a century.

We walked back into the cool of the château. The church bells rang to mark the *midi*. The scent of Carol's *poulet et morilles au vin jaune* came from the kitchen. We gathered at the dining table for a lunch that lasted all afternoon and into the evening, as Jean Claude and Bob reconstructed the astonishing story of their secret war.

PART
ONE

1

In the spring of 1944, outside the farming hamlet of Sussac in south-central France, an old water mill, long disused, rumbled back to life.

The mill was housed in a rock hut built right over a gentle stream feeding the Combade River. Screened by brush and trees, the hut looked abandoned from the dirt road outside, its windows frameless. In addition to its wooden waterwheel, though, the hut contained minimal furnishings—a chair, a table, two bedsteads with dubious mattresses, a stone sink that drained outside into a hedge. This was now the temporary home of a man identified in his official papers and ration books as Claude Jean Guyot.

Guyot's documents showed him to be a twenty-seven-year-old French office boy employed by an agronomist in Toulouse. He was of medium height and build, though unusually fit. As if to dial back the striking effect of his looks—fine nose, strong chin, brown eyes set wide apart—the photograph on his identity card showed him with his necktie and collar awkwardly askew. His clothing was tailored in the contemporary French manner, down to the buttons and stitching. His spoken French was accentless.

But he was, in fact, an American agent—the wireless operator for an elite team running a covert campaign of sabotage, subversion, and

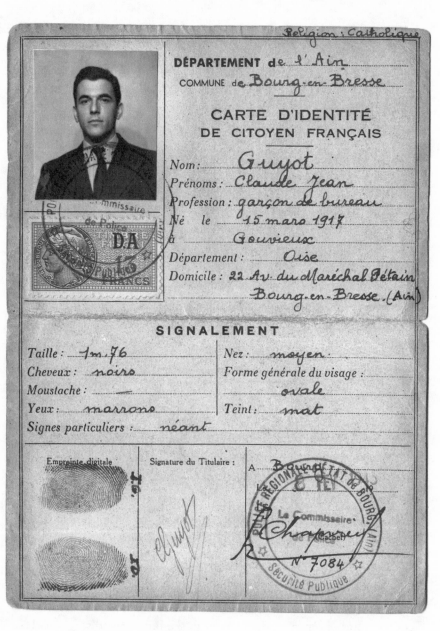

SOE forged a French identity card for "Claude Jean Guyot" with
Jean Claude's actual birth date but a false birth year, and his real
fingerprints, as well as a certificate of residence to verify his cover story.
The documents passed muster when examined by the Nazis.

CERTIFICAT DE DOMICILE

Je soussigné Mme. Rodel
Propriétaire, Gérant ou Concierge (1)

demeurant 30, rue Denfert Rochereau

certifie sous ma responsabilité que M Guyot, Claude Jean

est domicilié depuis mars 1943

Rue Denfert Rochereau   Nº 30

Le   21   avril   1944.

Signature et Cachet du Commissaire de Police du quartier.   Signature.

VU seulement pour certification matérielle de la signature de Mme Rodel le 22 avril 1944 Le Commissaire de Police.

J. Rodel

LAMY-TROUVAIN

ambush against the German occupiers. His real name was Jean Claude Guiet; his real age was twenty. The slow turning of the old waterwheel was vastly improving his life expectancy—measurable, as he well knew, not in years, or even months, but weeks.

The Germans, by that late stage of World War II, had become very good at radio direction finding. The Nazi *Funk-Horchdienst,* or listening service, monitored the entire radio spectrum between 10 kilocycles and 30 megacycles from a facility near Paris. Any frequency in use anywhere in France showed up as a spot on one of three hundred softly humming cathode-ray displays there. If a new, unfamiliar spot appeared, its frequency would be called in to three direction-finding (DF) stations on the country's periphery, which would fix on the signal instantly and pinpoint it within a triangular area about ten miles per side.

Then the hunt would begin. The first step was to momentarily shut down the electrical power grid, one substation at a time, in the zone identified. If the spot blipped off and on, it meant that the radio drew power from that substation. Then technical teams operating mobile DF stations, often carried in disguised laundry trucks but also sometimes in cars or small planes, would take over and narrow the field to within two hundred yards of the transmitter. Finally, if necessary, Gestapo men on foot, using sensors hidden under coats, antennae looped around their necks, eyes on meters disguised as wristwatches, would close in.

In 1944 the procedure, from the detection of a signal to the dispatching of DF vehicles, took as little as fourteen minutes.

Wireless operators were special prizes for the German military, as they were the vital link between Resistance fighters and the London spymasters who supplied arms, ammunition, and money by moonlight parachute drops. Captured agents were supposed to either swallow their L-pill (potassium cyanide, the *L* standing for lethal), or, if they could not, to remain silent for the first forty-eight hours of interrogation, giving their fellows time to get clear. The risk was never far from Jean Claude's mind: His reason for being there was that the team's previous radio operator had been captured months earlier near Rouen.

Jean Claude's borrowed water mill was a superb spot for operating his wireless set—a medium-power suitcase transceiver—as it offered both concealment and an off-the-grid power supply. Helped by an electrician friendly to the Resistance, Jean Claude had disconnected the heavy millstone from the waterwheel's shaft and propped it against the hut's wall. Then the two men had rigged belts and wooden gears to the shaft, the last belt stretched tightly over a pulley driving a small generator. The system amplified the slow turning of the waterwheel to a rate sufficient to charge a pair of scrounged 12-volt car batteries, which powered the radio. A long copper wire, threaded through a cracked roof tile and strung up into the branches of a tree, served as an antenna.

Even so, Jean Claude knew he was in peril every time he switched on his set. DF trucks occasionally roamed the countryside. A small plane flew overhead with unsettling regularity (most likely a German courier, Jean Claude thought, but possibly not). Worse, one member of Jean Claude's four-person team, Violette Szabo, had been captured and handed over to the Gestapo in Limoges. Who knew what information they might have extracted from her?

There was no question of curtailing radio transmissions, though; wireless traffic, like the tides, was determined by the phase of the moon. Only when the moon was more than half full was there enough light for the bombers from England to make nighttime parachute drops of war matériel. Then there might be four or five drops a night, each one requiring coded radio communication with London. For agents on the ground in France, as one later put it, "the moon was as much of a goddess as she ever was in a near eastern religion."[1]

Early one morning in July, as Jean Claude was preparing to leave the rock hut to help clear an especially large delivery from a drop zone nearby, he heard the sound of an engine. It was approaching fast, which in itself was alarming, as nearly all the French motor vehicles in the region had by that time been converted to run on charcoal, which reduced horsepower by about a third. Jean Claude peered through the hedge in front of the hut. Out on the dirt road he caught a terrifying glimpse of *feldgrau,* the German military's shade of gray.

He hurtled through the empty window at the back of the hut, just as a truck carrying German soldiers pulled up in front. Jean Claude sprinted about twenty yards and dove for cover in some thick brush. Soldiers leaped from the truck and stormed in through the hut's front door.

2

Before he figured out how to wire up the mill, Jean Claude had sent a coded message to his handlers in London requesting some kind of independent power source for his transceiver. They responded by sending him, in a canister dropped by parachute, a miniature steam engine. It was essentially a weaponized toy, green with polished brass accents, built to military specifications by the Stuart Turner model engine company in Henley-on-Thames.

Jean Claude took it out into the yard, filled its eight-inch boiler with water, lit a fire of twigs in its minuscule firebox, and spent the next few hours feeling a little foolish—listening to it chug, refilling the boiler, and tending the fire. He found that the engine, hooked up to a small generator, would indeed charge batteries, but so slowly that he would have to spend all his time tending to its tiny appetites for water and fire. A local French boy happily accepted it as a gift.

Deploying a toy steam engine to a war zone might seem like a quixotic military decision, but it was entirely in character for the British organization in which Jean Claude served, the Special Operations Executive. Sometimes called Churchill's secret army, SOE was as inventive as it was enigmatic, willing to try anything that might serve to terrorize Nazis.

SOE was one of the best-kept secrets of World War II. It was a volunteer organization operating outside the bounds of international law. Officially it didn't exist. On the rare occasions when it had to be mentioned in documents, it went by the name Inter-Services Research Bureau. It employed warriors, engineers, cryptographers, forgers, actors, murderers, burglars, and thieves. It was set up to give the British government deniability for its agents' actions, which were sometimes heroic, occasionally disastrous, and often shocking. After the war, generals on both sides expressed the view that SOE's activities had shortened the conflict in Europe by about six months, saving many thousands of lives.[1]

SOE was an important progenitor of modern special forces. As the historian Mark Seaman writes, "While France and Germany made a huge investment in military leviathans such as the fortifications of the Maginot and Siegfried Lines, Britain, in contrast, was seeking to explore the radical potential of clandestine warfare."[2] More than one scholar has noted that as an imperial power, Great Britain had broader experience with guerrilla tactics—because it had to defend against them—than most nations.

Yet SOE was neither an intelligence service nor a military special operations group. It was unlike any organization that has existed before or since, an underground militia with global reach, dedicated to sabotage, assassination, and—especially—armed resistance in every region of the globe occupied by the Axis powers. Its field agents, carefully chosen and trained, were scholars of mayhem.

For all its accomplishments, SOE remains far less well understood than other clandestine ventures that contributed to the Nazis' defeat, like the development of radar, or the breaking of the Enigma code at Bletchley Park. That's partly because of the wholesale destruction of its records. Researchers in Britain have combed through what remains, but they haven't had much to work with: an estimated 87 percent of SOE's original archive no longer exists. Outside the U.K., national pride has also helped keep the memory of SOE relatively obscure. Countries that fell under Nazi occupation have naturally celebrated their homegrown resistance movements and played down the contributions of outside agents. In France especially, the Gaullist mythology of the Free French has all but excluded SOE from history books. Charles de Gaulle himself, less than a month after his triumphal return to Paris in 1944, was introduced to a British SOE agent and told him, "You have no business here. Go home."

And yet there is no doubt: While resistance movements around the world had plenty of heart to stand up to the Axis powers, it was SOE that gave them teeth and claws. Thanks to SOE's work, when the Allied invasion of Western Europe finally came, it was aided on the ground by a large, coordinated guerrilla campaign—a first for modern warfare. As the Supreme Allied Commander, General Dwight Eisenhower, put it in a letter in 1945:

> In no previous war, and in no other theatre during this war, have resistance forces been so closely harnessed to the main military effort. . . . I consider that the disruption of enemy rail communications, the harassing of German road moves and the continual and increasing strain placed on the German war economy and internal security services throughout occupied Europe by the organized forces of resistance, played a very considerable part in our complete and final victory.[3]

As totalitarian regimes are wont to do, the Nazis called resisters "terrorists." In the case of SOE, they were sometimes not far wrong; this too has likely contributed to a certain fuzziness in recollections of the organization and its exploits. Agents who wrote memoirs in some cases understated the savagery of what they were called upon to do.

Jean Claude was one such memoirist. He wrote an account of his extraordinary wartime experience for his children and grandchildren, and gave it the title "One Man's Lovely Little War." It is forthright, but demure, with many upsetting and lurid events omitted for the sake of the grandchildren. And yet the present volume owes much to it. Wherever, in the pages that follow, there are descriptions of things that Jean Claude saw, heard, said, or thought, readers may be assured that they are not liberties taken in hindsight, but details set down by the secret agent himself.

SOE was a child of desperation, born in one of the darkest periods of the twentieth century: the summer of 1940, after the fall of France crushed the hopes of antifascists, but before the Battle of Britain revived them. The shadow of the Third Reich extended over nearly all of Europe, and Adolf Hitler was preparing to launch Operation Sea Lion, as he called his plan to invade Great Britain. Winston Churchill, the newly appointed prime minister, ordered the formation of a sabotage agency to take the fight to the enemy. (He gave the job of drafting its charter to the ailing Neville Chamberlain, notorious for his appeasement of Hitler at Munich in 1938. As Foot observes, "By a nice irony, Chamberlain's last political act was to devise a tool for felling Hitler.")[4]

Churchill put his minister of economic warfare, Hugh Dalton, in charge of the new secret service with a famous instruction: "And now, go and set Europe ablaze." To his chiefs of staff, Churchill gave a slightly more explicit order: "Prepare hunter troops for a butcher-and-bolt reign of terror."

By the time Jean Claude enlisted in the buildup to D-Day, SOE had about five thousand agents in the field worldwide, and another eight thousand support staff at home in Great Britain. It had two large secret radio stations, weapons laboratories, commando schools, a hidden airfield, and fleets of trawlers and caïques from the Shetland Islands to Ceylon. Its workshops devised an arsenal of deadly inventions, from the exploding rat to the one-shot cigarette to the Welrod assassin's pistol, so effective that it remains classified to this day. Some of these novel weapons were devised to attack conventional military targets, like the submersible, motorized canoe that agents used to attach limpet mines to ships. Others were plainly instruments of terror, intended to instill dread in the occupiers. Many German soldiers traveled by bicycle, so SOE devised an exploding bicycle pump. An agent coming across a German's unattended bicycle would swap out the pump and deflate the tires. When the soldier returned to find his tires flat, he would attach the pump, press on the handle, and have his hands blown off.

The goals of SOE's operations ran the gamut from relatively trivial—slipping itching powder into a shipment of shirts bound for a U-boat crew—to momentous: It was SOE agents in Norway who destroyed the German heavy-water plant at Vemork, thwarting Hitler's drive to create atomic weapons. SOE agents also assassinated Reinhard Heydrich, the SS general who was called—by Hitler himself— "the man with the iron heart," and who convened the Wannsee Conference to plan the extermination of Europe's Jews.

Occupied France was, of course, a major theater of operations for SOE. In the course of the war, SOE dropped ten thousand tons of weapons into the country. As Foot writes, "Arms are to active resisters what rain is to farmers—nothing can be done without them—and SOE was often the only serious source of supply."[5]

In the early war years the weapons were used mainly for sabotage. SOE infiltrated agents with false identities into France to establish networks—"circuits," as they were called—of brave French men and women willing to attack military and industrial targets. Train engineers were given grease guns rigged to inject abrasives into bearings. Factory workers and sailors were given lumps of coal with explosives inside, to drop into the fireboxes of steam engines. Sentries vanished.

As D-Day approached, and Allied troops massed in England for Operation Overlord, the Normandy invasion, SOE's mission changed. Now, the Allied commanders thought, was the time for massive, armed insurrections by Resistance fighters to aid the advancing regular troops. But they would need weapons, supplies, training, and leadership. Galvanizing these secret armies, deep behind enemy lines, became SOE's job.

How Jean Claude ended up in this harrowing role is one of those strange tales arising from the organized chaos of warfare. He was a draftee who happened to speak idiomatic French. And he was a big admirer of the tall leather boots issued to paratroopers.

3

SOE's F Section, which ran missions into France, had a custom: When agents were sent into the field, just before departing they were given an object made of gold. Female agents received a powder compact; men were given a fountain pen or a pair of substantial cuff links. The gifts served a double purpose. They were easily convertible to cash, should the need arise. And they reminded agents that SOE considered their lives precious, in spite of what it asked them to do.[1]

F Section was frank with its agents about the peril they faced, telling recruits that their chances of coming home were about even. Certainly the mission it assigned to Jean Claude and his team sounded improbable, if not suicidal: The agents were sent to block an entire Panzer tank division—an elite corps of the Waffen SS—from pushing north to Normandy and driving the D-Day invaders back into the English Channel. They were to do so by raising a guerrilla army deep inside occupied France, in the serene countryside around Limoges.

Prominent among the indignities inflicted on France by the occupation was the *Service du Travail Obligatoire,* or Compulsory Work Service. Under that program, signed into law on February 16, 1943, French workers were deported to Germany as forced laborers. Facing that prospect, hundreds of thousands of Frenchmen simply went to ground, living in hiding in the countryside. They became known as *maquisards*—the word *maquis* translates roughly as "scrubland."

Theirs was a precarious existence. Hunted by Nazis, they lived as woodland nomads, moving their encampments frequently. They relied on local farmers and villagers for food and supplies, but occasionally they had to resort to thievery, and some of their countrymen regarded them as little better than bandits. Civilians found to be aiding them were subject to murderous reprisals by the occupiers.

To avoid capture and deportation, the *maquisards* took up what arms they could—usually no more than hunting rifles and handguns—and organized themselves into embryonic resistance cells. In Brittany in the north, the Alps in the east, and the Limousin in the south, they undertook hit-and-run attacks on German troops. They helped Jews escape the country and gave assistance to downed Allied airmen.

The *maquisards* were, naturally, a diverse and loosely organized bunch, drawn from all social strata, with political affiliations covering the whole spectrum—then exceedingly broad in France—from monarchists to anarchists. Those belonging to the Communist Party had better cohesion and discipline than most. Others declared allegiance to de Gaulle and his Free French government-in-exile.

As D-Day approached, commanders in London—especially Churchill, an enthusiastic proponent of unconventional warfare—envisioned the *maquisards* as the shock troops of a general French uprising against the occupiers. If they were to be effective, though, they would need to set aside factional differences to focus on the common enemy.

SOE tackled the challenge by parachuting agents, shortly before and after D-Day, into regions of France where *maquis* groups were thought to be concentrated. Typically it sent agents in groups of four. One was an organizer, responsible for giving tactical direction and smoothing over political differences among the fighters. One was a courier—often a woman, who would be less likely than a young man to arouse suspicion at checkpoints. One was a wireless operator, and one was a sabotage instructor. Though they depended on one another for their lives, the agents had elaborate false identities; they didn't even know each other's real names.

SOE sent sixty of these teams into France during the invasion year, 1944. That was double the number of circuits it set up in 1943, when its operations were still focused on small-group sabotage. (In 1942 it established twenty-one circuits, and in 1941, six.)

Jean Claude's mission was code-named Operation Salesman II. The name itself had no particular meaning—SOE randomly used words for trades or vegetables or other things for code names, randomness being the essence of security—but the Roman numeral did. This was the second mission undertaken by the Salesman team. The first Operation Salesman had done some spectacular damage to the Nazis, but it had not ended well. The three survivors—the little band with whom Jean Claude went to war—had come through that first mission battle hardened and scarred.

THE ORGANIZER

Philippe Liewer was a mild, steady man who had seen a great deal in his thirty-three years. Born in Paris in 1911, he was educated at the *École Libre des Sciences Politiques*, which provided an interesting foundation for what he would eventually be called upon to do. Sciences-Po, as it is called, was established after France's humiliation in the Franco-Prussian War with the explicit aim of producing a new, technically skilled political elite.

Philippe studied journalism there, and after graduating in 1936 he was hired as a foreign correspondent by a French news agency. Two years into that job he was assigned to cover the Munich Conference, at which the major powers of Europe signed the treaty permitting Nazi Germany to annex the Sudetenland, as the ethnically

German regions of Czechoslovakia were called. Hitler expelled him from the conference because he was Jewish. Weeks later he enlisted in the French army.

When war broke out, Philippe served with an Allied expeditionary force, made up of British, French, and Polish troops, that was deployed in the so-called Norwegian campaign against the Germans in April 1940. He fought in the battle of Narvik, a grim struggle in snowy terrain for control of the port city, which was vital for the transshipment of iron ore. The Allies took the city, but shortly afterward they withdrew. Allied commanders, shocked by German military successes in France and the Low Countries, needed troops closer to home, and the Norwegian campaign collapsed. It was British discontent over this outcome that led to Chamberlain's resignation as prime minister and his replacement by Churchill.

Returning to France, Philippe served as a liaison officer with the British Expeditionary Force. That army quickly found itself trapped by German troops along the northern coast, near the border with Belgium. Philippe was rescued in Operation Dynamo, also known as the Miracle of Dunkirk, the evacuation of Allied soldiers from the beach by British volunteers in private boats—the "little ships"—that could get close to shore in water too shallow for the Royal Navy's destroyers.

After France surrendered to Germany on June 22, 1940, Philippe returned home from England and settled with his wife, Maryse, in Antibes, in the unoccupied *Zone Libre* governed by the puppet Vichy regime. There, in the summer of 1941, he was introduced to a pudding-faced man described as an English officer doing propaganda work. Philippe was suspicious at first, as the man spoke perfect French, but was reassured by the discovery that he spoke English with a strong Whitechapel accent. Philippe knew him as Touche; his real name was George Langelaan. He was a fellow journalist and writer who, later in life, was best known as the author of "The Fly," the short story on which the horror film was based. At the time he was an agent of the nascent SOE. Before slipping into France he had had his ears surgically pinned back, as they were too memorably prominent for clandestine work.

Supposing that Philippe's journalistic contacts might be useful, Langelaan hired him to help with propaganda and serve as a courier. Within a month, though, Langelaan was betrayed and arrested at a café by the Vichy police. Philippe's name was written in a notebook in Langelaan's pocket; the police found it and went to arrest him too. Philippe bluffed for about three hours, but when the police threatened to jail his wife he gave in and confessed that he had a connection with a British secret agent.

Philippe was taken to Beleyme prison at Périgueux, known as the worst of the French internment camps, where Langelaan and nine other F Section agents were being held in brutal conditions, subject to daily torture and near starvation. A few months later all eleven men were transferred to the Mauzac prison camp nearby.

The barracks where they were held at Mauzac had a door that was visible from a guard station and illuminated at night. Using smuggled tools, a mold made of bread, and a bit of tin, one of the agents fashioned a key to fit the door's lock. Another made a canvas replica of the door itself. At three o'clock on the morning of July 16, 1942, the men draped the canvas over the doorframe to hide what they were doing, opened the real door with their key, and slipped away into the night.

It took Philippe two months of arduous travel to make his way to Lisbon, where he found passage on a ship bound for England. In London he made contact with SOE, which signed him up and put him through its extraordinary course of training to become a full-fledged agent. The conditions of his imprisonment had left him unfit for parachute training, but otherwise he was deemed ready to serve. A report by one Sergeant Holland concluded:

This student is very intelligent and by virtue of his past occupation extremely well informed on all aspects of the political scene in France during recent years. He has a pleasant personality, is patient and scrupulously fair in argument and comment, and detests inefficiency and bad organization. In talks with me he has shown clear insight into all problems of security, to which he has obviously given considerable thought. . . . He has confidence in his own judgment, and speaks almost perfect English.[2]

THE COURIER

Violette Szabo is remembered in film, in biographies, and in the museum bearing her name as a ferocious warrior whose spirit the Nazis couldn't crush, though they gave it a good try. It is perhaps surprising, then, that her first assignment for the war effort was to pick strawberries.

Violette was nineteen at the time, still known by her maiden surname, Bushell, and living with her French mother and English father in London. After France was invaded in the spring of 1940, she signed up with the Women's Land Army. Land Girls, as they were known, took over agricultural jobs left vacant by men called up by the armed forces. Violette was deployed to Hampshire to help with the strawberry harvest. She liked the work, but once it was done she felt the need to make a more direct contribution to the war. She left the WLA and went back to London to look for one.[3]

She was already a crack shot. She grew up poor—her mother was a dressmaker and her father worked intermittently as a driver, car salesman, and factory hand. As she rarely had money for cigarettes, she developed the habit of visiting the many shooting galleries in the West End where cigarettes were given out as prizes.[4]

Violette was an athlete, a beauty, and a tomboy. She was raised with

Violette Szabo, in an undated portrait.

four rowdy brothers and a band of male cousins. She had jet-black hair, prominent cheekbones, a puckish sense of fun, and a strong competitive streak. She excelled at gymnastics and long-distance cycling, but she didn't care much for school; she dropped out at age fourteen. She was bilingual, as her family had lived in France when she was a little girl.

In that fateful summer of 1940, London was home to a large population of French refugees—soldiers and civilians who had fled their country ahead of the advancing Germans. On July 14, Bastille Day, the Free French held a parade at the Cenotaph in Whitehall, the U.K.'s national war memorial. Violette's mother sent her there with instructions to find a homesick French soldier and invite him for a family dinner and some conversation in his native tongue.

Violette returned with a sergeant major in the French Foreign Legion, a thirty-year-old of Hungarian extraction named Etienne Szabo. He, like Philippe Liewer, had fought at Narvik, returned briefly to France, and then been evacuated to London.

The dinner was a great success. As he left, Etienne asked Violette if she would like to meet again. She assented, and before long they fell hard for each other. They had a short, intense courtship, knowing that Etienne would soon be sent off to fight somewhere. On August 21, five weeks after they met, they married.

The newlyweds had only a week together before Etienne's Foreign Legion unit was shipped off to Africa. Etienne survived battles in Senegal, Eritrea, and Syria. Violette took a temporary job as a telephone operator and stayed at her post through the Blitz. Luftwaffe bombs destroyed her telephone exchange, but she was off duty at the time.

In August 1941, Etienne sent a telegram saying he was coming back to England on leave. Violette rushed to Liverpool to meet his ship, and the couple had a second honeymoon. Before Etienne shipped out, Violette told him that she wanted to enlist in the women's branch of the

British army, the Auxiliary Territorial Service. After they bade farewell, Violette went straight to the ATS recruiting office and signed up. It was September 11, 1941. Soon enough, she was trained to operate a "predictor," an aiming device for a heavy antiaircraft gun. Violette—ranked a private, but called Gunner Szabo—was posted to Frodsham, south of Liverpool.

She had barely begun working with her gun crew when she discovered that she was pregnant. Reluctantly, Violette left the ATS and went back to London. On June 8, 1942, she bore a daughter, Tania Damaris Désirée Szabo. Violette placed the baby in the care of a nursery that had been set up to look after the children of service personnel.

Four months later, Etienne was killed by Rommel's troops in the Second Battle of El Alamein, the critical fight that turned the tide of the North African campaign against the Germans. He never met his daughter.

Violette was shattered—and enraged. She wanted to strike back at the regime that had killed her husband, but it wasn't easy to imagine how a young single mother could accomplish such a thing—until, that is, a letter arrived a few weeks later inviting her to a meeting at an office in Whitehall. It stated no clear purpose and was signed E. Potter, a name Violette did not know.

Violette went to the meeting on the assumption that it would be related to Etienne's pension. She was greeted in a starkly furnished room by "Potter," a slight man in his forties. His real name was Selwyn Jepson, and he was, like George Langelaan, a literary man with a sinister precinct of Hollywood in his future; his novel *Man Running* would become the basis for Alfred Hitchcock's 1950 movie *Stage Fright*. At the moment, though, he was F Section's senior recruiting officer.

It isn't known precisely how Violette came to Jepson's attention. He had a network of scouts in government ministries on the lookout for prospects who spoke French, and it seems likely that she was spotted by one of them while training as a gunner. What is certain is that

Jepson had a special interest in cultivating women for clandestine operations. "In my view, women were very much better than men for the work," he said after the war, in an interview at the Imperial War Museum. "Women, as you must know, have a far greater capacity for cool and lonely courage than men."[5]

In the meeting with Violette, Jepson broached the subject of dangerous work in France. Violette said she would be interested. She didn't disclose that she had a child.

One of Violette's biographers, R. J. Minney, spoke with Jepson many years later for his book, *Carve Her Name with Pride.* Jepson told him, "The loss of her husband outweighed everything, even her motherhood—desperation which I should have seen as weakness. But, as it turned out, she derived strength from her training and from integration with the small group of men and women with whom she was trained for the work. Indeed she reacted in this way to a remarkable degree and the death-wish business (which after all was in the comparative safety of her consciousness and not buried somewhere deep inside her) completely cleared up, and that was all I was really worried about."[6]

A few weeks after that initial interview, Violette was given a cover story and a uniform to go with it: She was made a subaltern in the First Aid Nursing Yeomanry, a voluntary corps for women. Then she was sent off to be trained as a secret agent.

THE SABOTEUR

Bob Maloubier was seventeen when the Germans rolled into Paris, a tall, strong, devil-may-care teenager who, like Violette, was more interested in athletics than in school. The household where he grew up in Neuilly-sur-Seine, a Paris suburb, was bilingual; both his parents had worked as language professors at Adelphi University in New York. Besides idiomatic American English and a collection of ragtime records, they had brought home to France a love of sports. Bob's older brother, Jacques, became a member of the French national track and field team. Bob was a bicycle racer, a gymnast, and a hockey player. He was a strong swimmer, so much so that later in life he became the founder of France's equivalent of the Navy SEALs, the *nageurs de combat,* or combat swimmers. (And in that capacity, incidentally, he coinvented the dive watch, with its watertight case, black face, big luminous numbers, and rotating bezel to keep track of elapsed time.)

When war broke out, Bob knew exactly what he wanted to do: escape to London, join the Free French, and become a fighter pilot. He tried three times to make it to England, but was stopped each time. So in January 1941 he switched directions and went to North Africa to enlist with the *Armée de l'Armistice,* the small French force that the Germans had permitted the Vichy government to maintain. His plan was to train as a pilot, get hold of a plane, and at the first opportunity fly it to Malta or Gibraltar to offer his services to the Allies.

Bob was sent to the air base at Bizerte, in Tunisia. As there were too many pilots and too few planes, he was assigned to guard duty. In November 1942, a time of shifting allegiances among combatants in North Africa, the German High Command lost faith in the Vichy authorities in Tunisia and began to fear that they might switch sides. On the night of November 8, German troops surrounded the Bizerte air base and assaulted it. Bob grabbed a bicycle and rode out through gunfire, heading for Algiers. After pedaling for a day, a night, and another day, he reached the outskirts of Bône, Algeria (now called Annaba), where he was astonished to see two men in khaki uniforms roar past on motorcycles. The make of the motorcycles—Nortons—and their direction of travel—from the west—could mean only one thing: The Allied invasion of French North Africa, Operation Torch, had begun.

Entering Bône in the afternoon, Bob came across a brigade of British troops. Some soldiers invited him to stop and join them for tea. Just as he dismounted, a wave of Junkers Ju 88 fighter-bombers flew in low and strafed the town. Bob curled up in the fetal position at the foot of a tree and endured a hellish storm of flying metal.

When the raid was done, British soldiers lay dead and wounded in the smoking wreckage of vehicles. "Anyone here speak French?" a voice called out. "I need local doctors!"

Bob offered his services. He put out the word for doctors and helped transport the wounded to hospitals. A grateful British major gave him a letter of recommendation and a safe-conduct pass. Thus credentialed, Bob pressed on to Algiers.

Algiers was a city in chaos. Its French colonial population was divided between Vichy sympathizers under Admiral François Darlan, a notorious pro-Nazi, and Free French resisters, who had smoothed the way for the Operation Torch invaders.

Bob fell in with a group of Gaullists being trained as commandos, under British supervision, at a farm twelve miles out of town. Among them he was surprised to find an old friend from his Neuilly neighborhood, an earnest young monarchist named Fernand Bonnier de La Chapelle.

At the farm, the men trained with explosives and learned to use Sten guns, the cheap, simple, temperamental submachine guns that were produced by the thousands in England and were fast becoming the short-range weapons of choice for resistance groups worldwide.

Twice a week a British major named Jacques de Guélis visited the camp to teach marksmanship and unarmed combat. He was a large, jovial man who always seemed to have a pipe between his teeth, and he made a big impression on Bob. On one of his visits he stood with his hands in his pockets and said, "You, Bob, attack me."

"If you will not defend yourself, I cannot," replied Bob, who had taken boxing lessons in his school days from a world featherweight champion, André Routis.

"It's an order," de Guélis said.

Bob threw himself at the officer, and instantly found himself on the

ground, on his back, with a knee on his chest and a pair of hooked fingers inches from his eyes. "You have much to learn," de Guélis said.[7]

Bob applied himself to his training. He turned out to be particularly
good at shooting on the run. After a time de Guélis took him aside and
asked him if he would consider joining a branch of the British secret
service. Bob said no, he wanted to become a fighter pilot, but he agreed
to think it over.

As it turned out, he didn't have much choice. Admiral Darlan arrived
in Algiers on a personal visit, and Bonnier de la Chappelle and a group
of his Free French friends decided that it was an opportune moment to
assassinate him. They drew straws to decide who would pull the trigger;
Bonnier drew the short one. On Christmas Eve he went to Darlan's office and killed him with two shots from a Ruby 7.65 pistol.

Bonnier was arrested on the spot, interrogated, and executed on
Christmas Day. The day after that, Vichy police stormed the training
camp looking for his friends. Bob slipped away and located de Guélis.
The major offered to smuggle him out of the country—on the condition that Bob sign up with the organization he worked for, SOE.

4

In the autumn of 1943, shipwrights completed the refit of a German minesweeper at a yard on the river Seine, near Rouen. It was a small warship—900 tons displacement, with a crew of forty-five, a single main gun, two machine guns, and three antiaircraft "pom-poms"—but it was especially vexing to the Royal Navy. Used by the Germans as a submarine tender, it proved adept at slipping through the Allied blockade to deliver food and water to U-boats, allowing them to remain at sea for long cruises. British warplanes found it and damaged it, but they failed to sink it. The ship was taken to Rouen for repairs, and now, in early September, it was ready for sea trials.

Officers of the *Kriegsmarine*, the Nazi admiralty, boarded for a shakedown cruise of about four hours down the Seine and back upstream. Everything worked; champagne corks popped; the yard manager was handed a check for 5 million francs. At 5:00 that afternoon the crew began loading 20 tons of ammunition and supplies. They finished around 9:00 P.M. and went back to their barracks. Steam pressure was maintained at 5 kilograms in anticipation of a 4:00 A.M. departure.

Along with the crewmen loading stores, a French shipyard worker went aboard in the afternoon, saying he had to make a last-minute adjustment. It was a significant one: The man affixed a three-pound lump of plastic explosive, armed with two 6-hour timers, deep inside the hull.

At 11:00 P.M. the charge went off, tearing a five-by-three-foot hole below the waterline. The ship sank in six minutes. When Gestapo officers arrived in the morning, all they could see above the water was the tip of its smokestack.

The Gestapo men quickly decided that this was an inside job, and threatened to shoot all thirteen French workers who had had access to the ship unless one of them confessed. But then the *Kriegsmarine* sent its own divers to have a look, and on examining the hole they concluded that the charge must have been placed *outside* the hull. (The explosion was on the side of the ship next to a wharf; it is possible that the shock wave bounced, causing the misapprehension.) The French workers were released. A German sentry who had been on duty on the wharf was shot. When the forty-five crewmembers arrived and saw that they would not be putting to sea after all, they displayed unseemly glee. One of them was shot as an example, and the rest were sent to the Russian front.[1]

The scuttling was a high point of Operation Salesman—the first Operation Salesman—a ten-month reign of terror conducted by newly minted SOE agents Philippe Liewer and Bob Maloubier. Philippe had recruited the shipyard saboteur; Bob had given him the plastic explosive and taught him how to use it.

The Salesman agents were sent from England with orders to sow destruction from Rouen, Normandy's capital, downstream to Le Havre, the port city at the mouth of the Seine, where the river meets the English Channel. It was a horribly dangerous place for clandestine work. Rouen was the wartime headquarters of the *Kriegsmarine* in France. Le Havre was inside the *Zone Interdite,* the Forbidden Zone, a twelve-mile-wide strip along the French coast that the Germans were furiously fortifying against the anticipated Allied invasion. More than one hundred thousand enemy troops occupied the region—soldiers, sailors, and Gestapo—and among the French civilians there were informers and collaborators. Banners with swastikas hung from public buildings.

Philippe was delivered into this viper's nest by a Lysander, the strange little plane that was SOE's preferred aircraft for discreet work. The Lysander had fixed landing gear, reverse-tapered wings, and an ungainly profile, and it proved too slow and vulnerable for its intended role as a fighter-bomber. But it had an ultralow stall speed—the plane could practically hover—that made it ideal for landing on short strips, such as farmers' fields.

Philippe arrived in France on the night of April 14, 1943. A wireless operator, Isidore Newman, joined him in July, also flown in by Lysander. Bob followed a month later.

Posing as a chartered accountant in search of new business, with a forged pass to the Forbidden Zone, Philippe carefully built up a network of 350 saboteurs. A dressmaker in Rouen agreed to let his shop be used as a letter drop. A garage owner offered his facility as a weapons depot, and his charcoal-burning trucks—*gazogenes*—for transport. Arms were typically hidden under the trucks' charcoal supplies, as the mess discouraged searches.

The Salesman team established safe houses in Rouen, in Le Havre, and in the countryside between. Newman had the use of four apartments for his wireless set, and moved among them often. Recruits were organized in small groups and instructed to use cutouts and letter drops to communicate. All were kept in the dark about the Salesman circuit's overall size and structure, except the man Philippe appointed as his deputy, Claude Malraux, half brother of the novelist (and Resistance fighter, and future minister of cultural affairs) André Malraux.

On the night of October 10, 1943, shortly after the sinking of the minesweeper, Bob led eight masked men to a factory in Déville-lès-Rouen where landing-gear parts for the Luftwaffe's formidable Focke-Wulf 190 fighters were manufactured. The high walls looked impenetrable. Bob went to a small side door, the entryway to a sentry's lodging, and banged on it.

"Police, open up!" he called.

A woman's voice answered, "My husband is not here, and he told me not to open the door for anyone."

"For the police, madam, you will open the door."

The lock turned, Bob drove a knee into the door, and the terrified woman was pinioned and bound. The saboteurs went through the apartment's back door into the factory. A French factory hand figured out what was afoot and showed them to their objective, the pumps supplying pressure for presses and hammers in the machine shops. Using plastic explosives and timed fuses, they blew up four of the six pumps. The factory was out of action for fifteen days, and ran at 50 percent capacity for the next six months.

Three weeks later, Bob sat in the Café Ripol in Rouen with lumps of plastic explosive under his armpits and between his thighs. He had instructions to blow up a power substation at Dieppedalle, but it was a frigid day and the explosive was half frozen, too stiff to mold into shaped charges. So Bob sat in the humid café, nursing a glass of calvados grog, until it softened.

At nightfall he and five of his men scaled the wall of the substation and made their way inside. They rounded up the guards and workers— as it was a Sunday night, only a few were on duty—and locked them up. They affixed eight lumps of Bob's thawed explosive to transformers and switches, lit a 45-yard fuse, and pedaled away on bicycles. The blasts put the substation out of action for six months.

The Salesman team carried on in this way at a lively pace into the winter. They blew up a submarine repair facility in Le Havre. They burned barges on the Seine carrying war matériel. They derailed a

German troop train, killing 196 soldiers and wounding several hundred more.

On the night of December 20 they ran into their first bit of bad luck. The moon was bright, and London had scheduled an arms drop. Bob set out for the drop zone on a motorbike. On the seat behind him was a Salesman recruit, a forger with an office job who had asked to see a bit of action.

Riding out of Rouen into the countryside, they were overtaken by a Mercedes sedan. It stopped short in front of them. The moment Bob braked to a halt, his rider leaped off and ran away in the dark. German soldiers got out of the car and demanded an explanation. Bob said he knew nothing, the man was just a hitchhiker he had picked up. The soldiers ordered Bob into their car, to take him to the police station in a nearby village for questioning.

One of the Germans tried to kick-start Bob's motorbike. The engine wouldn't catch. The soldier kept at it unsuccessfully and finally exploded: *"Französische Mechanik, Scheisse!"* ("French engineering, what shit!")

The soldiers ordered Bob to get out of the car and help. He mounted the bike and, pretending to retie a shoelace, reached down and opened the hidden fuel cutoff valve he had closed when he stopped the machine. He stood on the kick-start lever and the engine came to life.

A soldier climbed onto the seat behind him, pressed the barrel of a Luger against his neck, and told him to proceed to the village. The Mercedes followed.

When they reached the village square, the Mercedes stopped in front of the police station. Bob threw his motorbike into a skid. His rider fell to the ground. Bob picked up the bike and hurled it on top of the man, then sprinted away down a side street. Shots rang out. Bob made it about fifty yards before a 9mm bullet pierced his liver and lung.

In shock, Bob kept running. The street became a dirt path. He covered another third of a mile. Stopping to catch his breath, he heard barking in the distance. The Germans were coming after him with dogs.

Coughing and bleeding, Bob pressed on. He came to a canal and saw a chance to throw the dogs off his scent. The night was frigid, but he plunged in, waded across, and climbed up the mud bank on the opposite side. He lay down in the middle of a field. His clothing froze, and he prepared to die.

Much to his surprise, Bob awoke shortly before dawn. He struggled to his feet, walked nine miles to Rouen, reached his safe house, and collapsed. A doctor told him later that the freezing cold had probably stopped his blood loss, saving his life.

He lay near death in the safe house for days. His men didn't expect him to survive; their main concern was how to dispose of his corpse, as a coffin would be far too conspicuous. They made plans to fold up his limbs before rigor mortis set in, so that they could fit his body into a burlap sack and dispose of it.

But Bob rallied. SOE sent a supply of sulfa drugs in a parachute drop. Soon Bob was well enough to walk.

In February, Philippe Liewer was scheduled to return to Baker Street to brief his commanders and receive fresh orders. He took Bob with him to recuperate. They were picked up in a moonlit field by a Hudson, a nimble light bomber, and flown back to London.

That's when Operation Salesman ran into its second bit of bad luck, this one much worse.

Philippe left his deputy in Rouen, Claude Malraux, in charge of the Salesman circuit in his absence. It isn't clear exactly how the Gestapo found him. They might have picked him up at a letter drop and tailed him. Someone might have claimed the reward that was on offer for information about the recent rash of sabotage. Malraux might have been indiscreet: A report in the SOE archive notes that he "seems to have behaved in [Philippe's] absence in the most insecure manner, spending long hours in bars, and getting at least twice thoroughly drunk in public."

Whatever the reason, Gestapo agents arrested Malraux on March 7, 1944. They caught him with documents detailing Salesman's operations, compromising the whole circuit. The next day they came for Newman, the wireless operator. They seized his radio and codes before he could send off a warning message to Baker Street.

The F Section spymasters in London, unaware that anything was amiss, set about preparing the next phase of Operation Salesman— vitally important now, as the invasion of Normandy was just a few months away. They gave Bob a brief leave to recover from his wound, and then sent him to an SOE school in Hertfordshire for advanced arms training. They sent Philippe to the RAF station at Ringway, near Manchester, to receive the parachute training he had skipped earlier.

At Ringway Philippe met another agent who was finishing up her SOE instruction: Violette Szabo. She was limping, having sprained an ankle badly on one of her first jumps, but her spirits were high and she was eager to be sent into action. She and Philippe got along well, and it was decided that for her first assignment she should join the Salesman circuit as its courier.

F Section arranged for Philippe and Violette to be flown to France during the March moon. Through coded radio messages, a drop zone and time were fixed, and a reception committee was organized. Philippe and Violette boarded their plane and prepared for takeoff.

They were taxiing down the runway when the flight was canceled. Baker Street had received an alarming message from an SOE circuit many miles away from Rouen, in the Corrèze. It said that a woman named Catherine, Claude Malraux's girlfriend, had reported to agents there that the Salesman circuit was blown. The Germans were using Newman's radio set and his codes in a game of bluff. Had their flight departed, Philippe and Violette would have been delivered straight into the hands of the Gestapo.

5

Abruptly, the task before Philippe and Violette switched from sabotage to salvage. What had become of the Salesman circuit? Who had been arrested? Were the safe houses still safe? Had their weapons caches been discovered? Could the circuit be revitalized in time to carry out an uprising when D-Day came?

The Salesman territory was now too hot for Philippe. Wanted posters bearing his image and Bob's were posted in Rouen. F Section decided that Philippe and Violette would go to Paris; Philippe would remain there while Violette traveled on to Rouen, alone, to try to pick up the threads. They would set out as soon as the moon was full again, in April.

In the intervening weeks, Violette was given a refresher course in encryption at Baker Street. Like all agents, she had learned the basics as part of her initial training. Now she was sent for a tutorial with SOE's head of codes, a young genius named Leo Marks. Their meeting yielded one of the enduring artifacts of the Second World War—a love poem, of all things.

MARKS HAD DEVELOPED a fascination with cryptography as a child, when he broke a code his father invented for noting prices on books in his London bookstore at 84 Charing Cross Road. (If the address is familiar, it is likely because a play and movie by that name are set in the shop, Marks & Co.) He was drafted and trained in cryptanalysis with a small group of prodigies. The others were sent to Britain's main codebreaking center at Bletchley Park, where Alan Turing, the father of theoretical computer science, was cracking the German Enigma code. Marks, judged too much a misfit for Bletchley, was assigned to SOE, where he became head of codes at age twenty-two.

Marks made a point of giving agents a final briefing on coding before they were dropped into occupied territory. He was haunted by the knowledge that security lapses could have dreadful consequences. "If you brief an agent on a Monday, and on Thursday you read that he has had his eyes taken out with a fork, you age rapidly," he once said, recalling the fate of an SOE operative in Yugoslavia.

At the time, SOE used "poem codes" for communications. An agent in the field would use the letters of a memorized verse, usually one learned in school, as the basis for a substitution cypher. A message thus encrypted was radioed in Morse code to Baker Street, where cryptographers using the same poem would unscramble it.

Marks didn't like poem codes, as he thought them insecure. If an agent used a well-known verse, and the Germans decoded even one of his messages, they might find the underlying text in a book and read all his future traffic. SOE agents were using works by Shakespeare, Keats, Molière, Racine, and Rabelais; one even used the National Anthem, as it was all he could remember.[1]

Eventually Marks worked out more secure systems, but as a first step toward better safety he began giving agents poems he wrote himself. Most were doggerel, like this:

The boy stood on the burning deck
His feet were full of blisters.

He hadn't got them from the fire
But from screwing both his sisters.

When Violette presented herself in his briefing room for her refresher course, Marks was smitten. ("A dark-haired slip of mischief rose from behind a desk. . . . held out her hand, and smiled," Marks wrote in his wartime memoir, *Between Silk and Cyanide*.[2]) But he was dismayed to discover that she was incapable of encoding messages using her poem, a French nursery rhyme, without making spelling mistakes. He offered Violette a fresh poem, one he had written himself.

The previous Christmas Eve, Marks had lost the love of his life, a woman named Ruth, who was killed in a plane crash in Canada. On receiving the news, Marks went up to the roof of his building, briefly considered throwing himself off, and instead wrote the following:

The life that I have
Is all that I have
And the life that I have
Is yours.

The love that I have
Of the life that I have
Is yours and yours and yours.

A sleep I shall have
A rest I shall have
Yet death will be but a pause.

For the peace of my years
In the long green grass
Will be yours and yours and yours.

Violette took the poem home to memorize. Marks tested her a few days later, and found that with the new verse she could encode a two-hundred-word message in under fifteen minutes, flawlessly. In gratitude, Violette gave Marks a present, a miniature chess set she had won at a shooting gallery.

There the story might have ended; the poem was never intended for publication. But long after the war, in 1958, R. J. Minney's biography of Violette was made into a movie—also called *Carve Her Name with Pride*—starring Virginia McKenna and Paul Scofield (with a young Michael Caine in a minor role). The poem was made public in the movie. It caused a mild sensation, and it has since made its way into anthologies. Couples sometimes use it in wedding ceremonies. It is doubtful that many of them are aware of the poem's actual provenance.

ON THE NIGHT of April 5, 1944, just before the next full moon, Philippe and Violette boarded a Lysander at RAF Tempsford, a secret SOE air base in Bedfordshire. Over their civilian clothing each wore a flight suit with zipped pockets for a revolver, a knife, a flask, maps, and a compass. Violette carried forged papers identifying her as a commercial secretary domiciled in Le Havre, which would allow her entry into the Forbidden Zone.

They flew across the Channel and landed in a farmer's field somewhere between Chartres and Orleans. The next day they made it to Paris, where Violette boarded a train for Rouen.

Violette then spent three harrowing weeks tracing the remains of the Salesman circuit. She dropped old passwords into conversations with strangers, contacted the wives of resisters, and chased the ghosts of spies in a city crawling with secret police and collaborators. Each meeting carried the danger that someone might betray her, if only to gain lenient treatment for a loved one being held by the Germans. Twice Violette was taken in for questioning by Gestapo agents, but her forged papers and her cover story held up.

What Violette found out was appalling: Nearly a hundred members of the Salesman circuit had been arrested. Philippe's lieutenant in Le Havre, a schoolmaster named Roger Mayer, had been beaten nearly to death by his captors. He had told them nothing, but one way or another the Germans had learned enough to roll up the entire operation. Claude Malraux, Isidore Newman, and most of the others were on their way to prison camps in Germany. Both Malraux and Newman were eventually executed in captivity.

Violette took a train back to Paris and gave her report to Philippe. He contacted Baker Street and arranged for them to be flown back to London. While they waited, Violette bought a silk dress with tiny pink and blue flowers against a white background for her daughter, Tania, then two years old, at a shop just blocks from Gestapo headquarters in Paris.

On the night of April 30, Violette and Philippe made their way to a small field near Châteauroux, south of Paris. SOE had two Lysanders operating that evening. Philippe boarded one, Violette the other. On the journey home, Violette's plane flew too close to an airfield at Châteaudun and drew antiaircraft fire, which shredded one of its tires. The pilot made it back to Tempsford and managed a safe, if violent, landing. He jumped out and opened Violette's door, and was taken aback when she let loose a volley of invective in rapid French. Violette imagined that the plane had crash-landed in enemy terrain, and that he was a German coming to apprehend her. When the pilot clarified matters, she threw her arms around his neck and kissed him.[3]

PART

—TWO—

6

While the Salesman agents confronted treachery and death in Hitler's Europe in 1943, Jean Claude Guiet, a world away in Cambridge, Massachusetts, was enjoying a thoroughly irresponsible year as a freshman at Harvard. He made a little money working as a waiter in a dining hall, cut lots of classes, and spent most of his time fooling around with an eccentric roommate. His grades suffered. If Jean Claude seemed to be the model of an immature college boy out on his own for the first time, that's just what he was.

Jean Claude's upbringing was bilingual, transatlantic, and sheltered nearly to the point of insularity. His parents, René Guiet and Jeanne Seigneur, met at the University of Illinois in Urbana, where both were exchange students from France. Their first child, Pierre, was born in Urbana and was thus an American citizen. Jean Claude was born three years later, in Belfort, France, and so began life legally French.

The Guiet family was formal, bourgeois, and well-to-do, though it reached that status by a curious route. René Guiet was the son of a postmaster in Saint-Briac-sur-Mer, on the rocky coast of Brittany. Serving in the French army during World War I, he was bayoneted in the neck and left for dead on a battlefield. Days later he was found by a farmer, taken to a nearby house, and nursed back to health. Rather than return to the army, René embarked on a moderately successful career as an art thief, according to family lore. He hid his collection, it was said, in an outbuilding near the house in Saint-Briac.

René had other talents, which came to the fore once peace returned. He was a superb violinist—later in life he performed occasionally with the Boston Pops Orchestra—and he was academically gifted. He obtained a doctorate from the Sorbonne in Paris, winning high honors for a thesis on French opera libretti, and embarked on a teaching career.

René's wife, Jeanne, was a strong and sometimes difficult woman. Born in Mandeure, in eastern France, she was attractive and socially ambitious, fond of giving elaborate parties. She was exceptionally bright and strong willed, but she had black moods and a vengeful streak. Expressions of love for her husband and children did not come easily to her.

In 1926 the Guiets settled in Northampton, Massachusetts, where René and Jeanne both took jobs in the French Department at Smith College (René eventually became the department's chairman). René sold some paintings and invested the proceeds shrewdly. The family lived comfortably in a clapboard house with a big garden on Washington Avenue, a leafy boulevard near the campus, with a French cook and two French servants. Jean Claude grew up without much exposure to ordinary American things; his principal playmate was his big brother, Pierre, and Jeanne insisted that the boys speak French at home. At the end of each academic year the family booked a first-class passage aboard an ocean liner—the *Normandie*, the *France*, or a Cunard ship—and went to spend the summer in Conliège, a farming village in the Jura, with a close family friend they called *Grandmère*. Jean Claude was unaware, until many years later, that he grew up in the Depression.

The family was not completely untouched by the outbreak of war in Europe. In 1939 Jean Claude was a fifteen-year-old day student at

Deerfield Academy; Pierre attended boarding school at Phillips Exeter Academy. That summer the boys boarded the *Normandie* and sailed to France as usual, but without their parents for the first time. In September, as they were getting ready to leave for home, war was declared. Pierre was eighteen, and even though he had an American passport, French officials wouldn't give him an exit visa. Because both his parents were French, the authorities considered Pierre French too—and eligible for the draft.

The Guiet family decided that both boys should stay with *Grand-mère* and attend a local school while the parents worked with the U.S. embassy to resolve the problem. Jean Claude and Pierre spent an enjoyable, rural academic year attending classes, chopping wood, feeding animals, and scything hay. This was the period of the "Phony War," when hostilities had been declared but shooting hadn't started in the West. Companies of reservists were quartered in the village, armed with ancient Lebel rifles with long bayonets that looked to the Guiet boys like fencing foils. But Jean Claude's biggest dread was the biweekly *dictée*, a dictation exercise in which pupils had to transcribe a text—underlining the title twice, without crossing any part of a letter that projected below the line—neatly in ink. It made Jean Claude long for a pencil with an eraser.

Early on the morning of June 15, 1940, a tremendous explosion shook the town. Gasoline storage tanks had been blown up to keep the fuel from advancing German troops. *Grandmère* and the boys lashed two mattresses, blankets, and suitcases to the roof of an old Renault and joined the throngs fleeing southward.

They found temporary lodging at a farm outside Sanssac l'Église, in the Haute-Loire department. They stayed in a single room that had been used to store barley, keeping their food in a box hung from the ceiling so the rats couldn't get at it. After two weeks they returned to Conliège; the Germans hadn't occupied the town after all.

The Guiet boys made contact with their parents back in the United

States, who sent money and made ship reservations for them out of Lisbon. Pierre had by then obtained a French passport, by the simple expedient of applying for it in a neighboring prefecture and not mentioning that he already had an American one. *Grandmère* was determined to stay at home, so the boys did what they could to prepare her for the hardship that lay ahead. They cut several cords of wood, gathered huge burlap bags of sawdust to burn in the stove if the coal ran out, dug up formal gardens to make vegetable plots, built two rabbit hutches, and laid in all the canned goods, sugar, and cooking oil they could find. Then, in mid-August, they packed two small suitcases and set out for Portugal.

They traveled by train to Barcelona, then on to Madrid. There they checked their suitcases and went to get something to drink in the train station buffet. Two members of the Guardia Civil entered and began checking everyone's papers. Pierre produced his American passport. The policemen saw that it had no Spanish entry visa, and they took the boys in for questioning.

Jean Claude and Pierre were locked in a holding cell with soiled, thin mattresses and a hole in the floor for a toilet. They spent three anxious days and nights there while the police and the U.S. embassy sorted out their case. Finally an embassy representative arrived at the prison with papers to secure their release. They returned to the railroad station, retrieved their bags, and boarded a crowded train for Lisbon.

Tickets were waiting for them at the offices of the American Export Lines. They boarded a freighter with passenger accommodations and large American flags painted on its sides, illuminated by spotlights, and sailed home.

Jean Claude settled back into his peaceable New England life. He spent the next two years at Deerfield. In the summers he worked on a farm, earning seven dollars a week and looking forward to the Friday night square dances at the local Grange Hall. When the United States entered the war after Pearl Harbor he thought about trying to join the navy, or perhaps the Free French, but he stayed in school and pleased his parents by doing well enough to earn admission to Harvard, where Pierre was enrolled.

But he wasn't ready for it. In his first semester in 1943 he worked long hours in the Dunster House dining hall, which was run like a full-service restaurant (he especially disliked it when students ordered grapefruit, which had to be prepared individually at the table). When Jean Claude had time to study, he usually didn't. In the second semester, Jean Claude made the dean's list—not the good one, but a list of students with dangerously unsatisfactory attendance records. He grew acutely uncomfortable at the thought of having to explain himself to his parents. So it was a relief when he opened his mail one spring day and found a draft notice from the U.S. Army.

7

"OK, you motherfuckers, drop your cocks and grab your socks, let's go!" That's what the corporal bellowed to awaken the troops on Jean Claude's first morning of basic training at Camp Croft, outside Spartanburg, South Carolina. Jean Claude remembered it for the rest of his life, because it was the first time he heard the word "motherfucker."

Jean Claude's journey into this new world began on June 9, 1943, when he was inducted and sworn in to the U.S. Army at a base near his home, in Fort Devens, Massachusetts. He spent a clamorous few days there—such was the chaos that he didn't recall exactly how many—signing papers, getting shots, waiting in lines, and tramping from one building to another amid shouts of "You'll be sorry!" from draftees who were only slightly less green. Then he was put aboard a crowded troop train for a journey of two days and a night to Camp Croft. The men ate their meals off paper plates in their laps. Windows were left open because of the heat, and soot from the engine blew in and made the mashed potatoes appear heavily peppered. Jean Claude learned to play cribbage and a little chess from a pair of Czech seatmates who had brought miniature sets.

Jean Claude rather enjoyed his three months of basic training.

There were the usual hardships—rising at 4:00 A.M.; KP duty; rifle practice in mind-numbing heat; guard duty in the middle of the night—but the regimentation was a pleasant change from the aimlessness he had felt in college. And Jean Claude had the happy realization that in addition to becoming a soldier, he was learning to be an American.

To Jean Claude, the men in his platoon were exotic: Italian Americans from Boston's North End, including one whose fine silk shirts and jewelry were taken for Mafia emblems; some genteel recruits from North Carolina, who explained to Jean Claude their theory of the "fairness" of racism; and a group of country fellows from Tennessee, one of whom caused a wild commotion by getting an erection during the platoon's first "short arm" medical inspection. In the evenings Jean Claude absorbed the stories they swapped in the barracks over fifteen-cent pitchers of beer.

Jean Claude was issued an M1 rifle, two sets of fatigues, a pair of boots, a canteen, a mess kit, leggings, a pack, a helmet, a helmet liner, and an entrenching tool. He was one of the few men who hadn't handled a rifle before, and he had difficulty disassembling and reassembling his weapon until a draftee who had been a state trooper gave him some tips. A sergeant advised the men to walk through puddles in their new boots to break them in and mold them to their feet.

The training was routine except for a pair of interruptions. First, Jean Claude was called off the firing range and driven in a truck to Spartanburg, where, to his delight, he was sworn in as a U.S. citizen. Second, he was taken to an office near the camp's headquarters and interviewed by a major—the highest-ranking officer he had met so far—who quizzed him about his French. The major asked if Jean Claude would be interested in some kind of special service, without elaborating, and gave him a sixteen-page questionnaire. Jean Claude filled it out, answering detailed questions about his family background, and mailed it in as instructed. He didn't give it a second thought.

At the end of basic training Jean Claude asked to be transferred to the U.S. Army Airborne School, for no particular reason other than that he admired the high-laced boots that paratroopers wore with their trouser legs tucked in. His request was granted, and he reported with his orders and duffel bag to Jump School in Fort Benning, Georgia. But after just a few days there—before his paratroop boots could be issued—he was called into the company office, given an envelope with new orders, and told to repack his duffel and be ready to leave in thirty minutes. He was driven to the train station, where he opened his orders and discovered that his destination was Washington, D.C.

Arriving in the capital early on a September morning, Jean Claude took a taxi as instructed to a building in a shabby neighborhood on E Street. He was escorted to an office on an upper floor, where a man interviewed him in French. The man's command of the language was very good, but he was not, to Jean Claude's ear, a native speaker. Jean Claude couldn't tell from his questions what the purpose of the meeting was, and he was too shy to inquire.

The man disappeared for a time, came back with some papers, had Jean Claude sign them, and welcomed him aboard the OSS. He told Jean Claude to take two weeks' leave, and then present himself in front of the Willard Hotel in Washington at 12:15 P.M. and "board the army truck" when it arrived. He stressed that Jean Claude was never to mention the OSS to anyone. Jean Claude found the admonition unnecessary, as he had no idea what the OSS was.

BEFORE PEARL HARBOR, U.S. intelligence services, like the military in general, were effectively dormant. Henry Stimson, serving as secretary of state, had gone so far as to close down that agency's code-breaking office in 1929 on the grounds that "gentlemen do not read one another's mail."

When war broke out in Europe, President Franklin Roosevelt—

who, like Churchill, had a keen interest in unconventional warfare—
was concerned about the muddled state of U.S. intelligence gathering.
Small operations were run separately by the army, the navy, the Trea-
sury, and the War Department, but there was no central authority for
collecting strategic information.

At the time, the British government had an office in Manhattan's
Rockefeller Center, on the thirty-sixth floor of the International Building. It was called the Passport Control Office, but in reality it was
the headquarters of Britain's top spy in the West, a man named William Stephenson. A friend of Churchill's, Stephenson was a charming,
Canadian-born millionaire who had been a fighter pilot in World War
I. His job was to gather intelligence, foil sabotage against Atlantic convoys, create anti-Nazi propaganda, and do whatever he could to persuade the Roosevelt administration to enter the war against Germany.

Stephenson cultivated the friendship of a Wall Street lawyer named
William J. Donovan, an energetic Irish American who also had served
with distinction in the Great War—the men in his platoon nicknamed
him "Wild Bill"—and made a fortune afterward. Donovan was an ad-
viser to Roosevelt; the two men had been classmates at Columbia
Law School. He was also something of an amateur diplomat who, between the wars, made several fact-finding visits to Europe and Asia.
He met privately with Churchill and reported back to Roosevelt (the
wheelchair-bound president sometimes referred to him as "my secret
legs"). Donovan became, in the words of one biographer, Douglas
Waller, "part of an informal network of American businessmen and
lawyers who closely tracked and collected intelligence on foreign affairs." Indeed, Waller writes, a friend recalled that Donovan was "not
happy if there is a war on the face of the earth, and he has not had a
look at it."[1]

Stephenson saw in Donovan an American ally who could help persuade Roosevelt to come to Britain's defense, and who, if given the
tools, could serve the president in much the same way he himself

served his prime minister. Stephenson arranged for Donovan to travel to England and receive deep, detailed briefings on the Secret Intelligence Service, better known as MI6, and on SOE. Donovan met with SOE commanders, reviewed tables of organization, and visited secret training camps and airfields.

In the spring of 1941 Donovan, aided by Ian Fleming, then a British Naval Intelligence officer, drew up a plan for an American spy service on the British model. Roosevelt received it enthusiastically, and on July 11 he appointed Donovan to the new post of coordinator of information. With $450,000 from a secret fund controlled by the president, Donovan set about creating the nation's first nondepartmental strategic intelligence organization. He found office space in a building at Twenty-fifth and E streets in Washington that was being abandoned by the Public Health Service. As Waller describes it, the building "still had caged lab animals the health service had used for syphilis research. Berlin radio mocked it as the new home of 150 professors, 10 goats, 12 guinea pigs, a sheep, and a staff of Jewish scribblers."[2]

Six months later came the attack on Pearl Harbor. Roosevelt put the new agency under the command of the Joint Chiefs of Staff, increased its annual budget to $10 million, and gave it a new name: the Office of Strategic Services. The OSS was to be responsible for intelligence gathering, psychological warfare, guerrilla operations, and the coordination of resistance movements.

To give his new agency a flying start, Donovan relied heavily on his undercover British friends. SOE sent instructors and training manuals. Donovan paid a visit to Camp X, an SOE school for assassins and saboteurs near Whitby, Ontario, and then had similar facilities built at two National Park Service campgrounds near Washington—one at Catoctin Mountain Park in Maryland, where Camp David is today, and one at Prince William Forest Park in Virginia, near Quantico.

The sites were isolated and heavily forested; they had water, electricity, and rustic cabins; they were owned by the federal government; and they were large enough, at thousands of acres each, for live-fire exercises.

OSS lore has it that ideal recruits were "Ph.D.'s who can win a bar fight" (the OSS Society registered that phrase as a trademark in 2016). At the outset, though, Donovan found agents much the way SOE recruiters did: by soliciting recommendations from friends in government, business, and academe, and supplementing their ranks with useful scoundrels. When the National Archives finally disclosed the names of OSS agents in 2008, it turned out that Donovan's "glorious amateurs," as he called them, included future Supreme Court justice Arthur Goldberg, historian Arthur Schlesinger Jr., philanthropist Paul Mellon, diplomat Ralph Bunche, poet Stephen Vincent Benét, major-league catcher Moe Berg, and author and chef Julia Child (who, at six foot two, was too tall for the Women's Army Corps). The quip that OSS stood for "Oh So Social" was not entirely unfounded; Donovan was, after all, looking for people with connections. On the other hand, "connections" means different things to different people. OSS reportedly hired men from Detroit's Purple Gang and from the Murder, Inc., crime syndicate.

Donovan understood that when it came to recruiting, the United States had a special contribution to offer for clandestine operations against the Axis powers all over the world. As John Whiteclay Chambers II writes in his history of OSS training methods, "It was one of Donovan's great insights that he could obtain from America's multi-ethnic population combat guerrilla teams that could successfully infiltrate enemy-occupied countries because its members spoke the language, knew the culture, and, in fact, were often the descendants of immigrants from that country. . . . OSS's Personnel Procurement Branch scoured training camps and advanced schools of all the services looking for intelligent candidates knowledgeable in a foreign language who were willing to volunteer for unspecified challenging and hazardous duty behind enemy lines."[3]

Though Jean Claude was still in the dark about all this in the autumn of 1943, he was exactly the kind of man the OSS was looking for.

8

Jean Claude stood anxiously in the Beaux Arts lobby of the Willard Hotel, directly across the street from the White House, at 12 P.M. sharp. He noted that other people in the lobby—some in uniform, others in civilian clothing—seemed to be waiting for something too, glancing out the windows now and then.

At 12:15 a large army truck pulled up outside. To Jean Claude's amazement, nearly everyone in the lobby filed out onto the sidewalk and began boarding the truck, talking shop, handing their passes to the driver. They were returning from weekend leave. It struck Jean Claude that whatever this clandestine service was, it wasn't all that discreet. He boarded too.

After an hour's ride the truck turned down a dirt road, passed through a security gate, and pulled up at a collection of rustic structures built in the 1930s by the Civilian Conservation Corps, which until recently had been a summer camp for low-income kids from Baltimore and Washington. Jean Claude would learn later that the OSS called this place Area C, for communications; it was the training site for wireless operators. It had new classroom and mess-hall buildings, but the sleeping quarters remained in their original condition: cabins with six cots each, windows with screens but no glass.

The passengers stepped down from the truck and the returning trainees drifted off, leaving Jean Claude standing with a small group of his fellow new recruits. They were taken to a classroom for orientation. The first rule, they were told, was anonymity: They were to address each other by first names only; ranks would not be mentioned. When several of the new men pointed out that their names were stenciled on their duffel bags, they were told to put the bags in the bottom of their foot lockers, out of sight. They were instructed to change into fatigues and report back in twenty-five minutes.

Escorted to a cabin, Jean Claude claimed a cot, changed his clothes, and buried his duffel bag in the unlabeled locker at the cot's foot. He returned to the classroom for more briefings that covered, in a general way, what OSS training was to be about.

When the orientation was done, Jean Claude stepped out the classroom door—and bumped straight into his brother, Pierre. Stunned, they both said "excuse me" and pretended to be strangers. A third man accompanying Pierre, who knew both brothers from college—the OSS was a very small world at that point—went through the charade of introducing them to one another by their first names.

It was an odd way for the brothers to learn that they had been recruited into the same top-secret organization, but it was probably intentional. Before reporting to Area C, each man had been granted a short leave and gone home to Northampton. Their leaves didn't overlap; Jean Claude's began one day after Pierre's ended. During Jean Claude's leave, Jeanne, their mother, told him that Pierre had mentioned that he would be stationed in the Washington area. Jean Claude replied that he would be too—of course never mentioning anything about the OSS. Jeanne expressed delight that her boys would be able to see each other in D.C.

What the Guiet brothers didn't know was that their mother had a secret of her own. Sometime in early September 1943—weeks before the brothers began their OSS training—a man described by Jeanne as

Pierre Guiet (*left*) and Jean Claude just before beginning their training at OSS Area C, whose protocol obliged them to pretend to be strangers.

"a general" had visited her at home in Northampton. Over afternoon tea, the man asked Jeanne how she would feel about having both of her sons recruited into a secret group to undertake dangerous work overseas in the war effort. Jeanne begged the general to take Jean Claude, but not her firstborn son, Pierre. The visit concluded with no commitment other than the general's assurance to Jeanne that her request would be conveyed and considered.

After the war, Jeanne told the story to Jean Claude without regret or defensiveness, explaining that in the region of France she came from, the eldest son was, by tradition, simply more highly valued than his siblings. She also said she believed that the general was Wild Bill Donovan. The story is family lore, and there is no official record of the general's visit or of deliberations about deploying the Guiet brothers. But in the end, Pierre served the OSS in the relative safety of an office in London.

At Area C, Jean Claude and Pierre were assigned to the same cabin—a situation that left Jean Claude scratching his head once again about OSS security. They saw little of each other, though, as they trained in different groups.

Jean Claude's three months at Area C were a far cry from his basic training. The OSS wanted its agents to be able to operate without orders—to think and act independently. At Area C there was no marching or saluting. In the mornings the men were awakened at 6:15, not by a drill sergeant's harangue but by popular music, often contemporary show tunes like "Oh What a Beautiful Mornin," played over the P.A. system.

The physical training was tough, intense, and scary, so for the sake of fitness and morale, the food was superb, at least for the military. The mess officer had been a restaurateur in Boston. He brought in fresh ingredients from the marine base at Quantico—chops, steaks, real eggs, produce—and prepared them to restaurant standards. He had his own bakery, and in the mornings the men had hot Danish and doughnuts. Huge refrigerators in a corner of the mess hall were stocked with food for them to take at any time.

The camp had pistol and rifle ranges, an obstacle course, a trench for grenade practice (to absorb shrapnel), and radio facilities. Paramilitary training covered weaponry, field craft, demolition, close combat, and "silent killing." In retrospect, Jean Claude viewed the curriculum as "the equivalent of a college survey course" in deadly skills: "We were introduced to many subjects but developed any real expertise in none."

It's possible that even many years afterward Jean Claude didn't fully grasp the high level of training he received. "A Major Fairburn of the Shanghai police taught us elements of hand-to-hand fighting," he recalled, "and how to use the Fairburn knife." That would actually have been William E. Fairbairn, one of the most fearsome martial artists who ever lived. He was sent by London to teach the OSS men how to fight dirty.

Fairbairn, a smallish, humorless, bespectacled Scotsman, had indeed served for more than thirty years in the Shanghai Municipal Police, battling gangs in the city's red-light districts. His arms, legs, torso, face, and hands were scarred from more than six hundred street fights, according to police records. He studied boxing, wrestling, savate, jujutsu, judo, and Chinese martial arts, and combined elements of them into a fighting method of his own, which he called Defendu. "I teach what is called 'Gutter Fighting,'" he said. "There's no fair play; no rules except one: *kill or be killed.*"[1]

By the time he arrived as an instructor at Area C, Fairbairn had acquired the nickname "Dangerous Dan" and had developed, among other things, the bulletproof vest, the riot baton, and the Smatchet, a "smashing hatchet" with a heavy leaf-shaped blade that some commandos reportedly found more useful than firearms for killing enemies at close quarters. His most famous invention was the one he taught Jean Claude to use, the Fairbairn-Sykes fighting knife, which he devised with a fellow Shanghai policeman, Eric A. Sykes. It was issued to British commandos and to OSS agents, and today it is featured in the insignias of special forces units around the world. The knife is a finely balanced dagger with a blade of seven inches more or less, depending on the production run. The length was chosen to leave several inches at the business end after the knife is thrust through a heavy coat. The blade is narrow, and slim enough to pass between ribs.

Jean Claude was taught to kill a person silently, thus:

Sneak up behind the target and place the left hand over the mouth. Shove the knife blade into the brain stem, just below the base of the skull. Give the handle a quick twist to ensure instant death. Leave the knife in place, to avoid blood spray, while lowering the body silently to the ground. Remove the knife and move on.

The Area C recruits practiced with dummy knives that had blades of stiff rope, rubber being scarce in wartime.

Fairbairn taught the men to fight without weapons, if necessary, using feet, knees, and elbows—but not fists. Open hands were much better, he said—the edge of the hand for slashing a neck, the base of the palm for smashing a nose, the thumb for gouging an eye.

Firearms instruction was another case of unlearning basic training. Fairbairn encouraged the men to forget about standard target marksmanship and instead practice "instinctive shooting," firing a pistol from a crouch or on the run with a two-handed, stiff-armed grip. He taught them to fire off two quick shots, and not rely on one—a practice that has come to be known as a "double tap." Using handguns of many calibers and nationalities, Jean Claude ran courses through the woods, shooting at targets as they popped up. Having barely made marksman at Camp Croft, he was surprised to find that he was rather good at this.

Many hours were devoted to guerrilla tactics, especially demolition. The men learned to handle black powder, TNT, plastic explosives, Primacord, and even flour—not actual flour, but a granular plastic explosive nicknamed Aunt Jemima. It looked like flour, and it could be pressed into shaped charges, but it wouldn't explode without a blasting cap. Agents carried it in flour sacks, and if caught with it they could actually bake it into muffins without risk (unless they ate the muffins).

The commando training was interspersed with lessons in spycraft. Jean Claude was taught how to steam open envelopes, and how to pick locks (though he never got beyond the three-tumbler variety). He practiced making and reading maps. He was introduced to the use of dead drops and invisible ink. For one whole week, the men in Jean Claude's group were told to invent a false identity for themselves and stay in character—Jean Claude put on a fake British accent. Twice the men were taken to the streets of Baltimore, once to practice tailing someone, and again to practice losing a tail. Jean Claude found it much harder than it looked in the movies.

The main subject of study at Area C, though, and the one that consumed by far the most of Jean Claude's time, was Morse code. Secure communications underpinned everything the OSS did, and by the autumn of 1943 the agency was training as many radio operators as it could, as fast as possible. Jean Claude was one of about two hundred at Area C—many of them ham radio enthusiasts in civilian life—receiving what amounted to a crash course.

At that point the war was at full boil, all around the globe. Allied armies, having conquered Sicily, were battling up the Italian peninsula. U-boats were taking a dreadful toll on Allied shipping in the Atlantic. Allied bombers were smashing Berlin; in retaliation, the engineer Wernher von Braun was designing the long-range V-2 rocket, the "vengeance weapon" that would be fired at Allied cities. The U.S. Marines battled Japanese troops in the Solomon and Gilbert islands, while U.S. and Japanese ships fought sea battles in New Guinea. That autumn, each side held a secret conference at which momentous projects were laid out. In October, at the Posen Conference in Poland, Heinrich

Himmler spoke to senior Nazi officials about the Reich's plans for Europe's Jews. He said:

"We were faced with the question: what about the women and children? I decided to find a clear solution to this problem too. I did not consider myself justified to exterminate the men—in other words, to kill them or have them killed—and allow the avengers of our sons and grandsons in the form of their children to grow up. The difficult decision had to be made to have this people disappear from the earth."[2]

The following month, Churchill, Roosevelt, and Josef Stalin held their first conference of the war, at the Soviet embassy in Tehran. The Allied leaders discussed campaigns in Yugoslavia and the Pacific, and the eventual creation of a United Nations. But the most important outcome was their joint decision to take a step Stalin had been pressing for since 1941: opening a second front against Germany by means of an invasion of France. The countdown to D-Day began.

As a rule, the American and British clandestine services operated in separate theaters of war. The OSS ran missions in China, Australia, Korea, and Finland, while SOE's territory included the Middle East, East Africa, India, and the Balkans. In preparation for D-Day, however, the two services formed a joint command in London, known as SOE/SO, with SOE as the senior partner. It drew on the OSS for recruits, including wireless operators from Area C.

Jean Claude found Morse training a bit tedious compared with the sabotage and combat exercises, but he turned out to be adept at it. He spent hours in a classroom learning the Morse alphabet, then sending and receiving messages through a closed system off the air. His transmissions were recorded and checked for accuracy and speed. The goal was fifteen to twenty words per minute. The instructors started Jean Claude off at a modest speed, and then, little by little, they raised it. Each time he reached a specified words-per-minute rate he would have a moment of triumph—and then feel like a frustrated beginner all over again when the rate was increased and the transmissions came in faster than he could handle them. By the end of his three months at Area C, Jean Claude had reached eighteen words per minute.

Jean Claude had already been spotted by the recruiters at SOE/SO. A letter of appraisal in his OSS dossier states: "Starting from scratch his progress in radio work was considered very good, and with the further training you will give him he should be a first-rate operator." It also states that Jean Claude "has given us the impression of being the brightest student in his class. He should distinguish himself in the field. . . . We believe him qualified to serve as a W/T operator and possibly as an organizer in France, and he specifically understands that he may be assigned to undercover work in that country."

His OSS coursework having concluded, Jean Claude was promoted to corporal. He readied himself to be shipped overseas.

9

At daybreak on December 28, 1943, a worn and well-traveled merchant ship converted into a troop carrier left New York Harbor, part of a large convoy bound for Britain. Among its passengers were Jean Claude; his brother, Pierre; and a small group of other OSS agents under the command of a master sergeant. It was not the kind of transatlantic crossing to which the Guiet brothers were accustomed.

The OSS men were segregated from the rest of the ship's company, confined for most of the twelve-day journey to a compartment without portholes on a lower deck. It was a big cabin, with green metal tables to port and starboard and a walkway down the middle. Each table had seating for eight, and meals were collected from the galley in pails, one pail per table. At breakfast, eight dollops of oatmeal would go into each pail, followed by eight hard-boiled eggs, then eight pieces of toast with jam. At dinner, the pail might contain eight servings of pudding on top of stew. The men would divide the food up at the tables using their mess kits.

They slept in hammocks slung three feet apart, swaying with the motion of the ship. In the daytime they were permitted on deck, where they could take in the reassuring sight of the convoy's many vessels, but the chill usually drove them below before long. The only other place available for their diversion was a windowless box of a structure set up near the stern, with a small canteen but no furniture, where soldiers squatted and joined in never-ending games of poker and craps in a thick haze of tobacco smoke. Jean Claude would go there to buy cigarettes. Once he was invited to take part in a game of poker, but knowing nothing about the game, he lasted two hands before he lost his money and quit.

The midwinter Atlantic was rough, and many of the troops became seasick. Then the plumbing froze. During the fifteen hours it took to repair the pipes, sewage and vomit overflowed from the ship's latrines.

About halfway across the ocean the engines quit. For five worrisome hours the ship wallowed in heavy seas. In case of torpedoes, the men stood on deck, in the bitter cold, wearing life jackets. A destroyer steamed in circles around them until the engines were restarted. The ship got under way again, and a day later it caught up with the convoy.

Several days after that, the ship was proceeding at dead slow speed through a dense fog bank. All at once the fog lifted, revealing the breathtaking sight of bright green hillsides and houses with red tile roofs. They had arrived in Greenock, Scotland. The troops disembarked on the quay, and Jean Claude had his first taste of English tea, in a cup handed to him by a woman in a Red Cross uniform.

Arriving by train in London, Jean Claude was picked up at the station by an American in an ammunition carrier and driven through the rain to Franklin House, a two-story mansion on the city's western edge. The house had a long drive, ample grounds, and a pair of stone lions flanking the steps up to the front door. It was owned by an American shipping magnate—some of its furniture was made with timber taken from his ships' luxury cabins—but during the war it was used by the OSS as its London reception center. Arriving just before dinner, Jean Claude was shown to a pleasant semiprivate room, and then he joined the assembled agents for drinks.

Franklin House was staffed by GIs, but it was informal and well appointed. The OSS men had no duties, their laundry was done for them, and they were served excellent meals at dining tables. Jean Claude had to get used to being waited on by men who outranked him.

After two days of this luxury, Jean Claude, Pierre, and some of the others were taken to an even grander estate, called Winterfold, in Surrey. This was not an OSS establishment, but rather the agents' first point of contact with SOE—not that they knew anything about it at the time.

Winterfold, a Victorian pile on several hundred acres, was the site of SOE's Student Assessment Board, which did the initial screening of recruits. Teams of psychologists, psychiatrists, and military officers evaluated each potential student's intelligence, fitness, emotional stability, leadership qualities, character, and values, but they didn't tell the students what they were doing or why. That's because some trainees were bound to wash out, and SOE didn't want them leaving with any knowledge of its methods, activities, or existence. Those judged unsuitable were sent for a sojourn at a comfortable country house maintained by SOE in the Scottish Highlands, nicknamed "the cooler," where they were encouraged to forget whatever they had seen and go home. Men with clipboards followed the students everywhere, taking notes but seldom speaking. They even observed the trainees sleeping, to see whether they talked, and if so whether they spoke in English, which could be fatal to any mission in occupied territory.

Early on in the war, SOE put each recruit through four weeks of this evaluation. With D-Day approaching, and the need for agents growing ever more urgent, the program was officially reduced to six days. For Jean Claude's OSS group it was three.

The first test, administered on their arrival just before teatime, involved looking at pairs of combinations of dots and dashes and determining whether they were identical. It was clearly a test of aptitude for Morse code. Jean Claude, with three months of Morse training and a slight propensity to show off, had no trouble with it. He learned later that some of the other OSS men did poorly on purpose, not wishing to stand out as potential wireless operators.

The next morning Jean Claude, along with five students he had not met before, was taken to a garden with a pond about thirty feet across. Scattered about the garden were odds and ends that might be found in an ordinary, if untidy, yard. The students were given a wooden crate the size of a footlocker, and a problem: They were to find a way to get the crate across the pond while remaining on the side they sent it from. The following rules would apply: the pond, though actually shallow, was to be considered unfordable. Swimming was not permitted, nor was walking around the pond. The men could use anything they found in the yard. The observer would answer questions before they started, but not after. There would be a three-hour time limit.

Questions were asked. What did the box contain? (Not pertinent, consider it classified.) Were the contents subject to damage by moisture? (Yes.) The observer started the clock.

Immediately, some of the men competed to take charge, a few of them loudly. Others stood to one side, contemplating the problem. Jean Claude and another man left the group and searched for useful items among the odds and ends lying about. From these it became clear that previous groups had tried to build a raft. They reported their finding back to the would-be leaders, who adopted the approach as their own.

With some fumbling and disagreement, the men made a raft that just barely kept the crate afloat. They still faced the problem of getting it across the pond. After some further argument they improved the flotation sufficiently to allow the smallest member of the group to stand on the raft. Then they debated how to use poles and lengths of rope to move the raft across the pond, unload the crate, and haul the raft back. They were just concluding that they could tie together shirts, undershirts, and trousers to make a sufficiently long rope when their time was up.

There was no debriefing. The men were told not to discuss the exercise even among themselves.

After lunch, Jean Claude and a different group of five OSS men were presented with a new problem. They were taken to a place on the estate's grounds where a dirt road passed through woods, with a steep embankment dropping off on one side. The road, they were told, was a frontier. A pair of armed guards, dressed in proper German uniforms, patrolled it.

The problem was to get an eight-foot wooden ladder, designated "a critical item," across the frontier and down the embankment without its movement being discovered. Attacking the guards was not permitted.

The OSS men conferred, collegially this time, and made a plan. They broke up into pairs to scout the "frontier" and determine the guards' routine. The road, they found, formed a gentle arc, bending away from them. The guards would meet in the middle of the arc, chat for a few minutes, and then walk back to the ends, where their view of its apex was limited. It took the guards about five minutes to reach the ends, and once there they would look on up the road for about thirty seconds before turning around and beginning the return leg.

Jean Claude was in charge of the three-person team elected to carry the ladder (three in case one tripped). Two other men were dispatched to watch the guards and give signals when they stopped to look down the road before turning around. They had to wait, tensely, for several repetitions of the routine before the guards stopped at precisely the same time. Then Jean Claude and the other men scurried across with the ladder, unseen.

The observers wrote on their clipboards, told the men not to discuss what they had done, and said nothing else.

The next day, Jean Claude was taken to a complex obstacle course. He was told to cross a theoretical pool of acid by jumping along randomly spaced stumps, each six to eight inches in diameter. Crossing in one part of the course, where the stumps were close to the ground, was worth a certain number of points; crossing in another part, with stumps one to three feet high, was worth more. When he had made it across, the observers quizzed Jean Claude about the decisions he had made in picking his route. There were half a dozen such exercises, evidently to gauge his physical capabilities and appetite for risk.

On the final day, Jean Claude was given the following problem: *You are part of an underground network, one of whose members has been arrested. There are some compromising papers hidden in his room. Find them and get them out.*

The person who gave Jean Claude these instructions also played the part of a nervous, pushy member of the imaginary underground network. Jean Claude started to ask him questions, to gather background information. What was the relationship between them? What was the layout of the room? What was the quantity and size of the papers? The man professed to know nothing more and urged him on, even pushing him. He said he would act as a lookout.

Uneasily, Jean Claude followed his directions: up three flights of stairs and down a corridor to the second door from the end on the right. He found a room with a bed, a dresser, a desk, an easy chair, and several bookshelves, with many books and magazines lying about. He looked first at the undersides of drawers, as he had been taught at Area C. He was starting to search behind the books on the shelves when the lookout burst in and announced that the German police were coming up the stairs.

Jean Claude said that in that case, he would simply walk down the stairs as if he were a resident. The lookout objected: The concierge, he said, was with the Germans and would not identify Jean Claude as a tenant. Jean Claude proposed going to the far end of the hall and acting as if he were about to enter his own apartment; or alternatively,

pretending to be a thief and going into any room that was open, bur-
glary being a lesser offense than espionage. He realized that while he
was talking, his lookout was hustling him toward a window. The man
urged him to climb out through it, crawl along the roof past a dormer,
and go down a fire-escape ladder that he said was just around the end
of the building. Jean Claude had no better plan, and the man's agita-
tion flustered him, so he complied.

He crept along a small ledge that held up the gutters, three stories
aboveground. When he reached the dormer he considered opening the
window and going back inside, but it was locked and he didn't feel that
he should break it. The metal ladder was a problem, as there wasn't
much to hold on to. But Jean Claude made it to the ground, where he
was met by a man with a clipboard, who made no comment.

Jean Claude felt like an utter failure. He hadn't found the papers,
and he hadn't resisted the lookout's instructions or insisted on more
information. That, he suspected, was what the test had really been
about: to see whether he would think for himself or do as he was told.

Jean Claude, Pierre, and the other OSS men were taken back to
Franklin House. They spent the better part of a week in idle luxury,
waiting for orders. Jean Claude spent much of his time exploring London via the Underground.

On the fourth or fifth day, Jean Claude was told to report to an address on Baker Street. It was a small, plain office building. In a sparsely
furnished office on an upper floor, he was interviewed by several men,
some in uniform, others not. They gave him forms to sign, verified that
his spoken French was idiomatic, and told him he would be attending
some special schools shortly. He was told he wouldn't be returning to
his OSS companions at Franklin House; he had no chance to say good-
bye to Pierre. The brothers didn't see each other again until the war was
over. Jean Claude was told to check into a small, inexpensive hotel two
blocks away from the Baker Street offices and to remain in contact
through a kindly, efficient lady called Mrs. Norris.

Jean Claude left with the conviction that he was "in"—but in what, he couldn't say.

In retrospect, Jean Claude believed that one of the men in the room was Colonel Maurice Buckmaster, the formidable head of SOE's F Section. Buckmaster—who before the war was a senior manager for Ford in France, gaining vast knowledge of the country's roadways and towns—made a point of meeting in person with every agent. And Philippe Liewer later told Jean Claude that while preparations were being made for Operation Salesman II, Buckmaster told the team members that he had found an American wireless operator for them.

Jean Claude spent several solitary days wandering around London. In the evenings he learned his way around the blacked-out streets. He didn't have the money or the nerve to respond to persistent and numerous overtures from the Piccadilly Commandos, as the West End prostitutes were called, so he retired to his hotel room alone.

Then one afternoon he was instructed on short notice to board a train for Morar, Scotland, for advanced commando training.

10

Behind the high walls of country estates taken over for wartime, SOE inventors developed an astonishing array of tools and techniques for deception, sabotage, and murder. At a mansion north of London called the Frythe, engineers developed the "sleeve gun," concealable under a jacket; a motorcycle small enough to be parachuted in a canister; several types of midget submarine; and the Welrod pistol, a foot-long assassin's gun so quiet that it remained in use through Operation Desert Storm (and probably is still used today, though the British government has never acknowledged its existence). In a London laboratory, a legendary inventor named Charles Fraser-Smith devised cameras hidden in cigarette lighters, hairbrushes containing maps and saws, and steel shoelaces that could be used as garrotes. For the screw-off top of a hidden document container, Fraser-Smith used the simple ruse of a left-hand thread; he explained that the German mind would never think to unscrew something the wrong way.

SOE's armorers were concerned with close combat, principally assassinations and ambushes, so they had little interest in mainstay infantry weapons like rifles. They focused instead on daggers, pistols, and especially the Sten gun, a cheap, inaccurate, ugly submachine gun. The Sten, like SOE itself, was born of desperation in the early days of the war: British troops left so many weapons on the beach at Dunkirk that the military faced the need for a firearm that could be produced quickly, in huge numbers, at minimal cost. The Sten had four parts—barrel, body, butt, and magazine—that could be stamped out by small manufacturers for thirty shillings. Its barrel was too short for any kind of accuracy, but it had a high rate of fire and could be devastating at point-blank range. The short barrel also made it easy to conceal; it could be broken down and carried in a rucksack. SOE distributed more than a million Sten guns in the course of the war, and they became potent symbols of resistance all over the occupied world.

Weapons of sabotage were a major focus of SOE's workshops, and among these, plastic explosives were probably the most important. Descendants of gelignite, invented by Alfred Nobel in the nineteenth century, plastic explosives had enough power to rupture steel but ordinarily wouldn't go off without a detonator. They could be dropped from airplanes, or carried over bumpy terrain, without fear of accident. Trained saboteurs could mold them into shaped charges for targets like bridges and railroad tracks. To give the saboteurs time to get away, SOE produced millions of "time pencils," just over six inches long, that could be pushed into a plastic charge and set for a delay ranging from ten minutes to a month. Pressing a ridge on the pencil released acid, which ate through a wire, which released a spring, which set off a detonator.

Perhaps the most notorious use of plastic explosive was the exploding rat. An SOE lab procured a hundred rat carcasses, skinned them, filled the skins with explosive, and sewed them back up. The idea was to drop a rat near the boiler of an enemy factory or ship; the carcass would likely be picked up and tossed into the firebox, where the intense heat would cause an explosion even without a detonator. The invention succeeded, but not as intended: The Germans intercepted a container of rats before they could be distributed, and it appears to have unnerved them. The rats were exhibited at German military schools, and a hunt was begun for suspicious rat carcasses all over the continent. An SOE report concluded that "the trouble caused to them was a much greater success to us than if the rats had actually been used."

SOE's lethal ambitions were global, so its craftsmen devised equipment for all theaters of war and all climates. For agents in the Far East they invented sandals that had the impression of a bare foot molded onto the bottom of the sole, so that footprints discovered at the scene of an ambush would appear to have been left by shoeless natives. For winter warfare they developed a tracked vehicle with an engine that would start easily in the cold. Called "the weasel," it was the ancestor of the snowmobile.

It was one thing to dream up and manufacture all these unconventional armaments; SOE also had to train agents to use them. Here again it relied on borrowed country estates. They were secluded, spacious, and easy to come by. Traditional country-house living was hard to keep up in World War II, most of the servants having gone off to fight. Owners tended to be more than happy to move out for a time and have the government pay for upkeep. By the time Jean Claude arrived in the U.K., SOE had taken over more than fifty estates for its special schools. It was sometimes joked that SOE stood for "Stately 'Omes of England."

JEAN CLAUDE STOOD ALONE, in fog, on the train station platform in Morar. His train had been full when it left London. When he changed trains in a big city—he assumed it was Glasgow, but he couldn't be sure because both city and trains were blacked out—there were fewer passengers. North of Fort William he was the only one left. He had been told he would be met at the station, but there was no one in sight. There weren't even any buildings besides the station house.

After a long five minutes a lorry loomed out of the mist. The driver offered a friendly hello, and that was the full extent of their conversation. There was no request for identification.

They drove several miles to a large estate called Rhubana Lodge, on the western shore of Loch Morar. It was one of ten big houses taken over by SOE in the bleakly beautiful, nearly deserted country around Arisaig, a village on the rocky west coast of the Scottish Highlands. The area had few roads, rugged terrain, and no inquisitive tourists: The Admiralty had declared it a prohibited area and closed it off. The "Arisaig Schools," as they were known, were where SOE did its advanced paramilitary training. If Jean Claude felt that his OSS instruction at Area C was like a college survey course, this was a series of master classes.

Rhubana Lodge, built in the 1860s by the Laird of Morar as a fishing lodge, had reception rooms, eight bedrooms, and kitchen facilities. Barracks and other outbuildings had been built on the grounds. Jean Claude arrived a little after 7 P.M. He was greeted by the duty officer, given supper, shown to his quarters, and told that training would start first thing in the morning.

He was awakened before dawn, issued a British battle dress uniform, and told to fall out for the "morning stroll." His group of trainees was divided randomly into pairs. Each pair was told to pick up an eight-foot-long, eight-inch-diameter log. Then they set off at a fast walk, with periods of jogging "to keep them awake," for an hour. Sometimes they traveled on narrow, hilly roads; other times they went across country. The logs were heavy and awkward to carry. The men had to learn to move at the same speed, find a common rhythm, and work out when and how to shift the load from side to side.

That morning Jean Claude got a painful case of shin splints. The "stroll" was repeated first thing each day, so it took most of the rest of the course for his legs to heal. The logs stayed with the men wherever they went. Moving to a classroom, firing range, mess hall, or barracks, they would pair off, pick up a log, carry it with them, and set it down again.

They spent a lot of time on small-arms training. Once sent into an occupied country they might have to use any weapon they could get their hands on, so they learned to handle British, American, German, and Italian pistols and submachine guns. They were taught to strip, reassemble, and load them in the dark. They trained with the excellent Anglo-Czech Bren light machine gun, with the American tommy gun, and, at great length, with the Sten gun.

Part of each day was devoted to practicing close combat. "Dangerous Dan" Fairbairn had set up the program at Arisaig and trained the instructors, so the drill was familiar to Jean Claude. He found that he preferred a combat knife called a Square Spike Sticker to the Fairbairn dagger. The Sticker, which was ten inches overall, had a thin six-inch blade less than a quarter inch wide, and could be worn in a sheath either on the belt or on the wrist. A training report sent by Jean Claude's instructors to Baker Street noted that he was "quick in action in silent killing."

Much attention was paid to the use of explosives, particularly of the British plastic variety. The men learned how to shape charges to blow a bridge or collapse a culvert. They had an excellent dinner one night—though they had to apologize for it—when one of them tossed a quarter of a pound of TNT into a stream and killed two good-sized salmon.

The main emphasis seemed to be on small group movement, getting from point A to point B, over and around obstacles, as inconspicuously as possible. In the open Scottish Highlands it wasn't easy to move about unseen, and the staff threw in complications. One day Jean Claude's group came to a small stream that they could have crossed on foot, scarcely getting their boots wet. But they were told to cross it using a rope that was stretched over the stream and hitched to a tree on either side. Some of the men tried swinging across hand over hand, but with the burden of their equipment the strain on their wrists was too much, and all but a few dropped off. The others remembered a lesson from a lecture the previous day: The trick was to lie down on top of the rope, hook one ankle over it, dangle the other leg outward and down for balance, grasp the rope, and pull oneself across. Jean Claude was surprised at how well it worked.

At night, the training covered the absolutely vital matter of running "reception committees" for parachute drops in enemy territory. Jean Claude later described that part of the Arisaig curriculum as "comprehensive." Parachute drops would be critical to Jean Claude's war—critical, indeed, to nearly everything SOE undertook. A concise description of how the committees operated is provided by M. R. D. Foot:

> They had to light and to guard the dropping zone, to guide any agents who were parachuted, and to dispose of parachutes and stores without a trace. Guarding and lighting were comparatively simple. Three men held torches or bicycle lamps out in a row, along the direction of the wind, in the middle of a flat space of open ground about half a mile across. The commander of the party stood with a fourth torch so that the lit torches looked from the air like a reversed capital L. When a distant rumble in the sky announced that an aircraft was near, all the torches were pointed towards it; the leader's torch flashing a previously agreed Morse letter. Provided the aircraft did see the lights and the letter was correct, it released its load above them and was gone as soon as it could, so as to attract as little local attention as possible.[1]

The training at Arisaig was fast-paced and tough, for it was both a course of instruction and a test of mettle. As many as a third of the students who went through it were judged to lack the grit for field work, and were sent off, with official thanks, to the cooler.

Those who made it through were customarily sent to "finishing school" at an estate in Beaulieu, near Hampshire. It was at Beaulieu that the SOE men and women were finally told what they had been selected and trained for. They were assigned elaborate cover stories and taught to live double lives, becoming, or at least appearing, as comfortable in their false personae as in their authentic selves. They were taught tradecraft: how to employ a disguise, lose a tail, use a dead drop, pick a lock, resist interrogation, and other unusual skills they would need to have a chance of survival as secret agents in enemy terrain.

Jean Claude was an exception. On completing his commando training at Arisaig he was sent directly to SOE's advanced wireless course, skipping finishing school. He was to be given his cover story in a special arrangement at Baker Street. No official record survives to explain this decision, but it's likely that because of Jean Claude's previous OSS training at Area C, it was felt that his progress through SOE's schools could be accelerated. What is certain is that by the late winter of 1944, SOE's trainers faced a momentous deadline. Jean Claude completed the course at Arisaig on February 19, 1944. It was 109 days before D-Day.[2]

11

Back in London, Jean Claude was granted a short leave that was notable only for a pair of small disappointments. He and a friend picked up two women in a pub, but as they were heading home together the friend passed out from drinking too much gin and orange, and Jean Claude had to look after him and call it a night. Another evening Jean Claude and an Italian American OSS man decided to splurge on dinner at Frascati's, a posh restaurant with a gorgeous marble grill room. They ordered lamb chops and were served mutton that tasted like soap.

After just a few days Jean Claude was taken to Thame Park, a grand estate in Oxfordshire where SOE ran its wireless school. The routine there was positively genteel—a far cry from Arisaig. Jean Claude was awakened each morning by a batman, a military servant, bearing a cup of tea. He would dress and go down to breakfast, spend the morning in classes, and have a long break for lunch. In the afternoon there were more classes, followed by a sort of high tea that served as dinner; Jean Claude relished slices of toast fried in bacon fat. The only drawback was the unremitting chill. There were radiators and fireplaces, but they were no match for the stone Tudor mansion's cavernous spaces.

The students frequently spent evenings in a warm village pub a mile away.

SOE wireless operators were nicknamed "pianists." The first order of business was to get their Morse speed up to twenty-five words a minute, both transmitting and receiving. Once they reached that threshold they were introduced to the set they would be using, a Type 3 Mark II radio. Housed in a small suitcase, it had three main parts: a power supply that could work on a variety of DC and AC voltages, a highly sensitive receiver, and a transmitter whose frequencies were determined by crystals. It was a little heavy to pass for an ordinary suitcase full of personal effects, but it had a range of some five hundred miles.

Jean Claude's Morse training at Area C had been in a closed, static-free system; now, for the first time, he was transmitting and receiving over the air. He was taught to tune his set as quickly as possible, and to limit transmissions to five minutes on any one frequency, to minimize the danger of detection by German direction finding.

Next came the all-important subject of coding and decoding messages. SOE had used several different encryption systems since the war began—including poem codes—and had discarded most of them as insecure or cumbersome. The notorious double transposition system, for instance, required that each message have a minimum of one hundred characters; that two numerical keys be used, each a different length; and that seven to ten dummy characters be added to the message so that the total number of its characters was divisible by five.[1] Asking agents to use such a code in the field, in haste, often in conditions of terrible stress, was not sound practice.

Mercifully, by the time Jean Claude had his piano lessons, the brilliant Leo Marks had persuaded SOE's spymasters to adopt a coding method that was at once simple to use and mathematically unbreakable. It was called the one-time pad, and it worked this way:

The agent in the field, and his handlers at the home station in London, had identical alphabetic tables for coding and decoding. The agent's table was printed on a silk square, like a handkerchief. Here is a photo of the table Jean Claude carried:

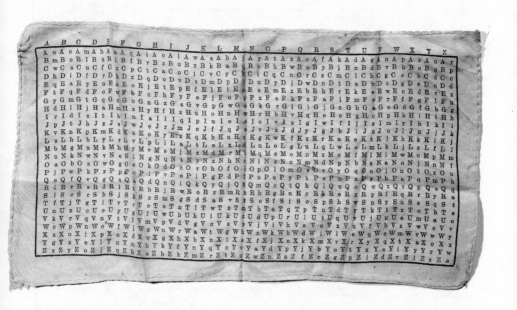

A standard alphabet ran left to right along the top. Underneath each letter was an alphabet running vertically, and, in lowercase type next to it, a randomly scrambled alphabet, also running vertically.

The agent in the field carried a small pad with pages of keys: five-letter groups of random letters. The home station had an identical pad. Each line of random letters would be used once, snipped off, and discarded—hence the name one-time pad. Here is a photo of a page from a pad that was issued to Jean Claude:

OUT STATION to HOME STATION

OUT STATION to HOME STATION

To encode a message, an agent used the pad and the table together. Let us say the agent wanted to transmit the message:

s e n d g r e n a d e s

He would write that out, and then he would turn to his one-time pad. Starting at the top left, he would write the letters from the first line of the one-time pad above the plaintext. If he used the pad in the photo above, he would get this:

YYINKRXIBWEY
s e n d g r e na d e s

Then, turning to his silk table, he would start with the key letter Y, go down that column to the letter *s*—the first letter in "send"—find that the code letter was *q*, and write it down. For the next letter in the message he would take the key letter Y, go down that column to the letter *e*, and find that the code letter was *v*. And so on. The result would look like this:

YYINKRXIBWEY
s e n d g r e n a d e s
q v t u p k d t e g n q

The agent would take the last, encoded line—q v t u p k d t e g n q—and send it by Morse code to the home station. The home station, using the identical key letters from a duplicate pad, would reverse the procedure to decode the message. Once the agent cut the top line of letters off the pad and destroyed it, the code could not be broken, even if an enemy got hold of the alphabet table.

The table was printed on silk so that if an agent was frisked, there would be no telltale crackle of paper. The pads were paper, printed with type so tiny it had to be read with a magnifying glass. Jean Claude carried his pads in a hidden compartment sewn into his wallet. Cutaway lines of key letters were supposed to be burned; Jean Claude found it simpler to eat them.

Each wireless operator was given his own security check to insert into messages, to confirm their authenticity. This usually took the form of a deliberate spelling error, such as replacing every tenth letter with the letter preceding it in the alphabet.

Jean Claude's orderly mind was well suited to this kind of work, and he excelled at it—so much so that the trainers at Thame Park didn't bother with his final exam. Jean Claude had been given to understand that the last exercise for pianists was a field test: They were expected to go to some English city with a wireless set, get a room, and meet a schedule of coded transmissions without being detected. But once again, SOE accelerated Jean Claude's instruction. Skipping the field test, he was whisked from Thame Park to the RAF air base at Ringway, near Manchester, for parachute training.

The decision to abbreviate Jean Claude's wireless training may have been necessary, but it substantially increased the risks to him and to fellow agents. At that very moment, SOE was suffering the deadliest setback in its short, eventful history, due to a lapse in wireless protocol.

The Germans called it *Das Englandspiel,* or the Game Against England. It began in March 1942, when an SOE wireless operator, H. M. G. Lauwers, was captured in the Netherlands by the Abwehr, the German military intelligence service. The Germans compelled him to send messages of their own devising to Baker Street. Lauwers omitted his security checks—he was supposed to garble every sixteenth letter—which should have alerted London that he was transmitting under duress. But somehow SOE's N Section, which ran operations in the Netherlands, missed the signal.

A German counterintelligence team, led by Major Hermann Giskes, exploited this opening for the next two years. The Germans sent coded messages to N Section requesting parachute drops of arms, agents, and additional wireless sets. Agents were arrested the minute their feet touched the ground, and thoroughly interrogated. Giskes eventually had fourteen SOE wireless sets exchanging messages with Baker Street. His penetration of N Section was so thorough that he knew which brands of cigarettes SOE instructors preferred. He sent daily reports to Hitler.

Leo Marks smelled a rat. He noted that the messages arriving from the Netherlands were immaculately coded, without the (actual) errors that could be expected from field agents operating in stressful conditions, and suspected that they were the work of enemy cryptographers. He devised a little trap. He knew that German wireless operators customarily signed off their transmissions with the letters HH, for Heil Hitler. He had one of his cryptographers send a message to the Netherlands and end it with HH. In an instant, as if by reflex, came the reply—HH.

Even so, Marks was unable to persuade his superiors that N Section was blown. It wasn't until two captured agents escaped from the Netherlands and sent an alarm from Switzerland that the ruse was detected. By then sixty-one Dutch and British agents had fallen into German hands; nearly all were shot.

Giskes wrapped up the *Englandspiel* with a message sent to Baker Street, in plaintext, on April Fool's Day 1944. It read:

> You are trying to make business in Netherlands without our
> assistance. We think this rather unfair in view of our long and
> successful cooperation as your sole agent. But never mind
> whenever you will come to pay a visit to the Continent you may
> be assured that you will be received with the same care and
> result as all those who you sent us before. So long.

12

Paratroopers played such a decisive role in the war that it is easy to forget that in Britain, at least, jumping out of airplanes was still considered a novelty when hostilities began. (Germany, and especially Russia, were miles ahead of the U.K. in this kind of combat.) Some of the early instructors at Ringway, in fact, were stuntmen from a "flying circus" air show. When Jean Claude arrived there, the school had grown into a massive operation—altogether about sixty thousand soldiers passed through it in the course of the war—but Ringway's training facilities still had a seat-of-the-pants feel, with wooden slides, pulleys suspended from ceiling beams, and mattresses for cushioning falls.

SOE men and women were kept apart from the other paratroop trainees, for secrecy and anonymity. Jean Claude and about a dozen other agents, none of whom he knew, were quartered in a large house near the air base with a walled garden and a two-story garage.

Immediately after their arrival, the students were taught how to fall: ankles together, knees slightly bent, hands over their heads, rolling to the right or left to absorb the shock. They practiced that for several hours. Then they moved on to a zip line with a twelve-foot drop, to practice the same maneuver with some realistic momentum.

The next morning they were escorted to the garage. Looking up, they saw that a round hole, four feet in diameter, had been cut in the second floor. Above it, affixed in the cupola, was a small drum with a cable wound around it, at the end of which was a harness. The drum had a pair of small paddles attached to it. The students climbed up to the second floor and were told to take turns strapping on the harness and stepping off into the hole. They were not given any other instructions. Jean Claude wondered how he was to avoid being maimed. He was astonished to discover that as the cable played out and the paddles whirled faster and faster, they created enough air resistance to slow his descent to a rate that made the impact of landing perfectly manageable.

Working with this rig, the students were introduced to the concept of controlling a parachute using the risers, the web strips that connect the harness to the parachute lines. They became familiar with the quick-release mechanism that freed them from the harness on landing. The most important thing they learned in the garage, though, was the proper procedure for exiting through a hole in the floor. That was how RAF planes were set up to deploy paratroops, as opposed to U.S. aircraft, which sent them out through a door. The students sat at the edge of the hole, and at the command "Action stations" they swiveled their feet into it. At the command "Go!" they pushed upward and out, careful to keep their bodies straight up and down. Leaning too far back could mean snagging a parachute; leaning too far forward could mean breaking a nose or losing teeth.

Just before teatime, the students were taken to a staging area to watch parachutes being packed. This, they were told, was to give them confidence, as they would not have a reserve chute. They were to be dropped at such a low altitude that they wouldn't have time to use one.

Early the next morning, dressed in jumpsuits, they were driven in a bus to the Ringway airfield. No one spoke much. They boarded a Whitley, a twin-engine medium bomber with a "Joe hole," as it was called, in its belly. The Whitley took off and flew above the airfield. It was Jean Claude's first time in an airplane.

At "Action stations," Jean Claude put his feet into the hole. He felt a mild tension at the sight of the ground moving by below. At "Go!" he went rigid and pushed off. He felt a jerk as his parachute was pulled open by its static line—only a gentle tug, as the Whitley was old and slow. There followed, he recalled later, "an exhilarating feeling of floating with no downward motion over a quiet landscape." He was aware of loudspeaker instructions from the ground, but he paid little attention, absorbed in the sensation of weightlessness.

Suddenly Jean Claude perceived that the ground was coming up at him very quickly. His feet touched, so lightly that he had to force himself to tumble. His chute collapsed easily, and he bundled it up and walked to the edge of the airfield, where he and the other students giddily compared notes on the wonderful feeling of seeming to hang motionless in the air. They had benefited from a complete lack of breeze; one of them, a small woman, even had trouble with the light morning updraft, and made a frustratingly slow and irregular descent.

The trainers told them that their performance was adequate for a first jump, but that they should pay more attention to preparing to land.

The next morning they repeated the exercise, this time full of confidence. They even sang bawdy songs on the bus. There was some wind, and when Jean Claude took his turn at the Joe hole he saw the ground moving diagonally. He kept his focus on the way down, but his body started swinging in relation to the chute. He tried to minimize the swing by the use of his risers, but he timed it wrong: When he reached the ground his feet were up at the end of an arc, not underneath him. He managed to roll, but he landed with a thump. He was impressed at how much effort it took to collapse his chute even with just a gentle breeze blowing.

The final exercise at Ringway was a nighttime jump. This was made not from a Whitley but from a tethered balloon. The balloon had a gondola big enough for six students and a dispatcher, with a Joe hole in the floor. As the balloon was let up, Jean Claude could see dim blue lights spaced along the cable, but he couldn't see the ground; there was no moon.

The dispatcher checked each student's static line to make sure it was clipped on correctly. Then he said casually, "You chaps know the drill well enough so you don't need me"—and jumped, leaving the students to their own devices.

Jean Claude decided that he didn't want to be the last to jump, so he went first. Because there was no slipstream from an airplane, his chute took far longer to open this time, and he had a horrifying feeling of freefall. Then he heard his chute deploy with a sharp crack. He didn't see the ground until seconds before reaching it. He managed to roll into a relatively soft landing and bundled his chute. Then he wandered around the darkened airfield, completely disoriented, until he heard voices. These turned out to belong to other students, who were just as addled by the experience as he was.

That night the SOE agents had a small celebration. The next morning Jean Claude left for London, and a new identity.

13

In the final weeks of May 1944, London had the curious distinction of being the world capital of trickery and deception. The Allied military, having chosen Normandy's beaches as the site for the D-Day invasion, devoted stunning amounts of manpower, money, and imagination to the task of fooling the German High Command about it.

The strategic puzzle was this: The Nazis had fifty-nine divisions, each made up of fifteen to twenty thousand men, in France, Belgium, and the Netherlands. The Normandy landings—Operation Neptune—would be the largest seaborne invasion in history, but the Allies were going to need crucial days, even weeks, to get soldiers ashore and build up the troop strength for a breakout. If the Germans managed to move enough tanks and infantry to the beaches in time, the invasion would fail.

The solution was not to try to conceal the Normandy operation altogether, but to persuade Hitler that it was merely a feint, and that the main force would be coming ashore elsewhere. To this end the Allied strategists, using fake radio messages and leaks through German double agents, created an entire fictitious army—the First United States Army Group, or FUSAG—massed around Dover for a fictitious landing at Pas-de-Calais, directly across the Channel. They put up phony mess tents, made dummy jeeps and planes out of wire and canvas, and planted bogus wedding notices for make-believe GIs in local newspapers. They built rubber tanks to deceive German spotter planes; a few real soldiers moved them around at night and used special rollers to create phony tank tracks.

They created another fictitious force, the British Fourth Army, based in Edinburgh, and spread the word that it would join with Soviet forces for an invasion of Norway. For this they generated spurious radio traffic about topics like ski bindings and cold-weather engine maintenance.

When they found an Australian actor who looked a lot like Field Marshal Bernard Montgomery, the Allied commander, they dressed him in one of Monty's uniforms and sent him to Gibraltar and Algiers. The hope was that Germans would spot him and conclude that a Mediterranean invasion was planned as well.

This vast campaign of misdirection was code-named Operation Bodyguard, a name taken from a remark that Churchill made to Josef Stalin: "In wartime, truth is so precious that she should always be attended by a bodyguard of lies." While it unspooled in a critical (and successful) game of strategic bluff, Jean Claude, in London, prepared for D-Day with a deception of his own: becoming a counterfeit Frenchman.

From an SOE staging area, Jean Claude was hustled around to secret facilities in plain-looking buildings devoted to the "activation" of secret agents. He was asked formally whether he was prepared to proceed, and when he assented he was given a physical exam and asked to write a last will and testament. The gravity of his situation began to sink in.

He was escorted to an old, derelict-looking warehouse where tailors with strong foreign accents coached him in choosing appropriate French civilian clothing. He selected underwear, socks, handkerchiefs, shirts, trousers, shoes, and a jacket, and was told to come back in several days to pick them up. When he did he found that all the items had been aged somehow. On close inspection they were not at all worn out, but they looked as if they had been lived in for a long time and laundered often. The shiny new leather jacket and the shoes had lost their gloss and stiffness and become scuffed and broken in.

The day after choosing his wardrobe, Jean Claude was honorably discharged from the U.S. Army as a corporal, and within the hour was promoted to second lieutenant, the lowest officer's rank. All SOE agents were given some kind of officer's commission in the hope that if they were captured, they might receive better treatment under the terms of the Geneva Convention than if they were enlisted men. As a practical matter it probably made little difference, because of the infamous Commando Order issued by Hitler in October 1942. That order stated: "From now on all men operating against German troops in so-called Commando raids in Europe or in Africa are to be annihilated to the last man. This is to be carried out whether they be soldiers in uniform, or saboteurs, with or without arms; and whether fighting or seeking to escape." The order was issued in secret, and only twelve copies were made, suggesting that the German commanders knew it constituted a war crime long before it was so judged at the Nuremberg trials.

In Jean Claude's case, capture would probably not mean immediate execution in any event. As a wireless operator he would likely be subject to the full horror of a Gestapo interrogation to make him give up his codes and contacts. In the circumstances, a much better protection than an officer's commission was a strong cover story, and Jean Claude's was prepared with elaborate care.

To minimize the chance of slipups under questioning, many elements of his story were close cousins of the truth. His name was changed from Jean Claude Guiet to Claude Jean Guyot. (He practiced his new signature, with a little flourish underneath, over and over.) The date on his false birth certificate was his actual birthday, March

15, though he was aged by seven years. Moving his birth year back to 1917 made it plausible that he had been discharged from the French military in 1940, as a corporal, having served with the 81st Battalion of the Alpine Fortress Infantry. His papers showed that before joining the army he had lived with his family in Lons-le-Saunier, a town he knew intimately, having attended the *lycée* there the year he and his brother had been stuck in France.

The fictitious Monsieur Guyot, after his discharge, lived at 22 avenue du Maréchal Pétain in Bourg-en-Bresse, another town Jean Claude knew from his youthful travels. In April 1943 Guyot moved to Toulouse, where he resided at 30 rue Denfert Rochereau and was employed as an office boy by Jean Leygue, an agronomy engineer. The work didn't agree with him, and he was now on the road looking for another job.

Guyot's fictitious parents bore the same given names as Jean Claude's own. The father, René, died in 1930. Guyot's mother, Jeanne, had taken up with several lovers and become a severe alcoholic. Guyot believed she was living in Senlis, but he no longer had much to do with her.

Jean Claude was given a portfolio of forged paperwork to support this story: Guyot's birth certificate, work certificate, identity card, food and clothing ration cards, and demobilization papers. The documents bore varied handwriting, an assortment of inks, and Jean Claude's fingerprints where appropriate.

Jean Claude spent long hours over many days internalizing his alter ego's biography, drilled by SOE instructors. They filled him in on details of places Guyot would have known about, like the Marseille train station, which he would have passed through on his discharge from the army. Twenty-five years later, when Jean Claude saw the station for the first time, he remembered it vividly.

In free moments during these busy weeks in London, Jean Claude relaxed by playing volleyball with other agents back at the staging area.

He and a man called Bob, playing hard games on opposing teams, struck up a friendship. Bob was about Jean Claude's age and spoke English with a pronounced French accent. He was a *sportif,* a natural athlete. The two began spending time together at the staging area— Bob seemed to have quite a lot more free time than Jean Claude did— and though they didn't disclose any personal information about themselves, conversing in French they found that they had much in common, particularly an easygoing outlook on life.

On May 21, the day after he received his second lieutenant's commission, Jean Claude was about to head out to buy his new uniform when he was summoned to Baker Street. He was shown to an office— a nearly bare space, as usual—where a man in a British major's uniform introduced himself as Charles Staunton. Major Staunton appeared to be in his late thirties and was slightly shorter than Jean Claude. He had an olive complexion, an amicable expression, and alert eyes that bulged slightly.

They began their interview in English. Jean Claude was struck by the major's aristocratic diction—and astonished, consequently, when Staunton switched to French and spoke it with an obviously native Parisian accent. They conversed in French about generalities, and after a time Staunton expressed relief and satisfaction that Jean Claude was clearly a native speaker too, unlike many other candidates he had interviewed. He said that Jean Claude seemed to fit his requirements, and that he was confident they would work well together. Jean Claude asked Major Staunton if he was a Frenchman, and he allowed that he was. Then he invited Jean Claude to lunch.

They went to a restaurant in Soho, a long, narrow, very noisy room crowded with mainly French military personnel. They found a table, and in short order they were joined by a tall man with a Clark Gable mustache in a Canadian captain's uniform, his cap set at a jaunty angle. Jean Claude was surprised to see that it was his new friend Bob. They pretended not to know each other at first, but soon dropped the charade. Bob and Major Staunton conversed like old friends, in French, which Jean Claude thought must be some kind of security breach considering the uniforms they wore.

Then a fourth person joined their party, a very attractive young woman in the uniform of an officer of the First Aid Nursing Yeomanry. Introduced to Jean Claude as Corinne, she clearly knew the other men well. She was small, a few inches over five feet, with long dark hair, a high forehead, and eyes that seemed to squint a little. Her movements were lithe and graceful, and her French was fluent, though to Jean Claude's ear it had the faintest trace of an English accent that might catch the attention of a very suspicious listener.

They had a pleasant lunch amid the restaurant's hubbub. Jean Claude felt himself gently drawn into their circle. Staunton no doubt had been thoroughly briefed on his background, but he gave no sign of it. Corinne was irreverent, insouciant, and fond of jokes. Jean Claude divined that Bob had had something to do with his being invited there.

Nothing was said about it, but Jean Claude had just joined the Salesman team. Major Staunton was actually Philippe Liewer. Bob was Bob Maloubier, now fully recovered from his chest wound. Corinne was Violette Szabo.

WITH ONLY A FEW DAYS left before his scheduled departure for France, Jean Claude got his jump boots at last. He received his officer's uniform too, though he didn't get to wear it, as the trousers took the better part of a week to tailor. The uniform, along with the boots, went straight to an SOE facility for storage during his "absence."

Jean Claude was asked to write four or five postdated letters that would be sent to his parents. He arranged for his pay to be deposited in an account at Chase National Bank in New York. With Mrs. Norris, he went over the proper use of his forged ration books.

Jean Claude's radio set was checked over thoroughly. He was given tiny one-time pads to carry in the hidden compartment in his wallet; the radio set included a small pair of scissors for cutting off used lines of code. He was also given his security signals—special characters that he was to include in every coded message to let London know that he was not transmitting under duress.

He was issued a worn-looking suitcase, into which he packed his French clothes.

He was offered an L-pill. He declined it.

14

On the evening of June 4, 1944, Jean Claude, Philippe, Violette, and Bob sat wearily with drinks in a country house north of London, singing a pop tune that was becoming a theme song for them, a hit ballad by the Mills Brothers called "I'll Be Around." ("I'll be around / No matter how / You treat me now / I'll be around from now on. . . .") The agents were winding down in Hassells Hall, a huge Georgian edifice, after a long, disappointing day. Hassells Hall was one of the residences attached to SOE's top-secret air base, RAF Tempsford—the jumping-off point for missions into enemy territory.

The Tempsford base was designed by a renowned London stage illusionist, Jasper Maskelyne, to resemble an abandoned farm, especially when viewed from the air. Its buildings had missing windows and roof tiles; barracks and hangars were disguised to look like run-down haylofts; old tractors were left here and there; and the two runways were painted with green and brown patches to appear overgrown with shrubs. There was a large farmhouse, shabby on the outside like the other buildings, but actually a state-of-the-art operations center linked directly to Baker Street.[1]

Behind the farmhouse was a barn where agents were given their final checks and instructions before taking off. It was there that the Salesman team had assembled earlier in the day.

Jean Claude had his orders. They read, in part:

> Our agent Hamlet [Philippe's code name] is returning to the field during the June moon period to take over a circuit which covers the Southern part of the Haute Vienne and parts of the Departments of Dordogne, Corrèze and Creuse. This circuit originally formed part of a larger organization, the chief of which was arrested at the beginning of May. His work is being carried on by his second-in-command, Samuel, but in view of the large area involved and the likelihood of communications becoming more difficult with the approach of D-Day, it has been decided to divide the circuit, and Hamlet is taking over the Southern area. . . .
>
> Your mission is to act as W/T operator for Hamlet and you will take all your instructions from him. . . .
>
> You will be parachuted into France . . . to a point 9 kms. N. of Chambert, 40 kms. E.S.E. of Limoges.
>
> You will be received by a reception committee organized by Samuel.
>
> Should you by any mischance miss the reception committee and lose contact, you can get in touch with Samuel through the following address:
>
> Mlle. Guillon
> 16 rue de la République
> Châteauroux
>
> Password: "Je viens pour une chambre."

Reply: "De la part de qui?"

Your reply: "De la part de François."

[Translation: "I've come for a room." "Who sent you?" "François sent me."]

In the barn, Jean Claude, Philippe, Bob, and Violette changed into their French clothes and lightweight jumpsuits. They were issued pistols and ammunition. Jean Claude's radio crystals were checked, and he was given a small cardboard box to carry them in on his person. The agents' pockets and wallets were inspected for anything that might compromise them, like English cigarettes or bus tickets. Their suitcases were likewise checked, and then packed, along with Jean Claude's radio, into canisters to be dropped with them.

Then they were told not to mention their pistols when they passed through customs.

They looked at each other. Customs?

Sure enough, there was a customs checkpoint by the door to the tarmac outside. An officer asked them if they had anything to declare, and one by one—wearing jumpsuits, carrying weapons, without luggage—they politely said no and passed through to the blustery airfield outside.

It remains a mystery why the customs ritual was put in place, but it had a salutary effect. The jokes the agents told each other—about what a person might actually have to do to get stopped at that checkpoint—helped them manage the rising tension they felt as they were driven to their airplane.

They boarded an RAF bomber in the dark. A dispatcher settled them on the floor and checked their parachutes. The plane began to move.

After just a few minutes it stopped. The agents assumed the pilot was waiting for clearance to take off, but then the dispatcher informed them that the flight had been scrubbed. The weather had turned foul, making it too dangerous to fly. Exasperated, the Salesman agents climbed out of the plane, went back through the barn, and returned to Hassells Hall for a nightcap and a wistful song.

The agents were far from alone in their frustration with the weather that night. In fact, the meteorological forecasts made on June 4, 1944, have become the subject of their own small field of scholarship, as the course of Western history was altered by them. June 4 dawned with bright skies over England, but a storm was detected moving eastward over the Atlantic. The D-Day invasion was scheduled for the next day, June 5. American weather forecasters predicted that a ridge of high pressure would steer the storm away from the English Channel in time. British forecasters disagreed, and advised the Supreme Allied Commander, Dwight Eisenhower, to postpone the invasion by one day. Eisenhower assented, and D-Day was moved to June 6. The weather did turn foul on the night of June 4, and remained so on the fifth. Some historians conclude that if Eisenhower had gone the other way and stuck with the June 5 invasion plan, his planes would not have been able to supply air cover, and the war's outcome would have been different.

The Salesman agents turned in for the night, the men sharing a room, Violette in a room of her own down the hall. In the morning they had an early breakfast in the dining room, which was crowded with commandos speaking different languages and wearing assorted military uniforms and civilian disguises. Having nothing to do until nightfall, they borrowed a car and drove to Cambridge, where they strolled about and had a pleasant lunch. In midafternoon they drove back to Hassells Hall and played blackjack, betting recklessly with British money they would be leaving behind. None of them came out a big winner.

After dark they went back to the airfield, passed through customs again, and boarded an RAF Lancaster bomber. This time the plane took off. The agents sat in the dark, subdued, talking only a little. They played a few more games of blackjack, gratefully accepted cups of coffee and hot chocolate provided by the dispatcher, and tried to doze.

All at once they were wide awake: the standby warning light flicked on.

Jean Claude felt a rising panic. The cardboard box containing his crystals was wedged underneath one of his parachute straps, but it kept sliding around. He tightened the strap until it made him hunch uncomfortably, but still he couldn't secure the box. If it came loose and fell to the ground, his crystals would scatter, the operation would fail, and he would be responsible.

Jean Claude was still wrestling with the problem when the cover of the Joe hole was removed. The agents sat around its edge, looking down at a landscape lit by a dim moon: woods, meadows, here and there a darkened village, small streams that glittered faintly. Jean Claude glanced at Philippe and saw the muscles of his jaw twitch; he was a little reassured that someone who had gone in before seemed to be just as nervous as he was. (Jean Claude didn't know then that this was Philippe's first operational jump too; his previous trips to France had been by Lysander.)

The plane circled for what seemed to Jean Claude like an eternity, though it was probably five to ten minutes. Then the dispatcher approached. The agents braced themselves.

The dispatcher informed them that there would be no jump—the reception committee had not shown up. (It had been run off by a German patrol, they later learned.) He motioned the agents away from the Joe hole. Before replacing its cover, he dropped carrier pigeons in special parachute cages. The hope was that French civilians would find the birds and use them to send back details of German installations and troop movements. Jean Claude wondered how many of them would end up in stewpots instead.

The agents loosened their parachute harnesses and relaxed. The trip back seemed much shorter than the outward-bound one. When Jean Claude mentioned to the dispatcher that he had never landed in an airplane before, he was escorted to the bombardier's station in the nose, where he watched the English countryside sloping up at him in the faint predawn. By four in the morning the team had returned to Hassells Hall and turned in.

Scarcely two hours later Jean Claude, Philippe, and Bob were awakened by someone pounding on their door. It was Violette, bearing the news that the invasion of France had begun.

BY THE TIME they made their third passage through the Tempsford airfield barn, the Salesman agents had become familiar to the customs officer, who waved them through with a friendly "good evening."

It was the night of June 7. This time their plane was a B-24 Liberator flown in from RAF Harrington, the airfield that was the base for Operation Carpetbagger, a joint venture by the OSS and the U.S. Army Air Force to drop supplies to resistance groups in Europe. Carpetbagger B-24s were specially modified for low-altitude nighttime work. They were painted black; had their nose guns, belly guns, and waist guns removed to gain speed and cargo space; and had blisters added to the cockpit windows for downward visibility. Where the belly gun used to be, they had a Joe hole.

The flight was pleasant, almost relaxed. Jean Claude had figured out a better way to carry the cardboard box with his crystals—inside his jumpsuit. The agents played blackjack and gin rummy in almost total darkness.

The warning light came on. The dispatcher hooked up their static lines and removed the plywood cover from the Joe hole. They sat with their legs dangling into it. Jean Claude noted that Philippe was looking up at the warning light with what seemed like studied nonchalance.

Bob stifled a yawn, perhaps a little theatrically. Jean Claude smiled at Violette. She winked at him.

They made a first pass over terrain that appeared more wooded than open. Jean Claude worried about getting hung up in a tree. The plane banked, turned, and made a second pass.

That's when the dispatcher called the mission off. He gestured to the agents to back away from the hole. In dismay, they complied. They started to unhook their static lines.

Then the warning light came on again. The bomber's engines throttled back, and the agents heard the command "Action stations." They secured their static lines and scrambled back into position around the hole.

They heard the "Go!" command. Philippe straightened up, pushed off, and jumped. As soon as his shoulders and head had disappeared, Violette followed him. Then Jean Claude, his body rigid, eyes shut tight, dropped into the night. Bob jumped last.

15

Jean Claude felt his parachute snap open, and an instant later his feet touched the ground—the drop was only six hundred feet, an unusually low altitude, to minimize hang time and reduce the chance of being spotted by a German patrol. He had no sensation of free floating. He managed a safe landing, got out of his harness, and unzipped his jumpsuit as the sound of the Liberator's engines faded away overhead. He saw no sign of the others. He had landed near trees, which meant that he must be at an edge of the drop zone.

The first order of business was to fold up his parachute. Jean Claude reached for his cardboard box of crystals to set it aside before bending down for that task. Drawing it out of his jumpsuit, he was horrified to feel the crystals cascading out into the thick, damp grass. One end of the box had torn open.

Jean Claude knelt and began feeling around, panicked. There were twelve crystals, each two inches square and half an inch thick, with two prongs at one end. In the space of a few minutes he found more than half of them. He was still on the ground, searching for the rest, when he heard voices. He looked up and saw the moonlit shape of a *kepi,* the flat-topped cap worn by French policemen, rising behind some bushes not far away. Then he heard the man say, loudly and emphatically, "I'm certain I saw one of them come down over here."

Jean Claude had not been told anything about policemen on the reception committee. He drew his pistol and cocked it.

At that moment Philippe's head appeared, right behind the policeman's shoulder.

Jean Claude stood up and called the men over. He explained his problem to Philippe. Together they found all but one of the remaining crystals, and Jean Claude stuffed them back into the cardboard box while the policeman folded up his parachute. It turned out that the local police, on hearing of the invasion, had joined the Resistance that very night.

Jean Claude and Philippe made their way over to the reception committee, where they were joined by Violette and Bob. The four agents were bundled into a police car and driven the few miles to Sussac, a tiny farming village. A truck followed with their suitcases and Jean Claude's radio, recovered from the canisters by the reception committee.

They stopped at a general store on a corner of the town square. Ordinarily it carried a combination of groceries and hardware, but at this stage of the war the shelves were rather bare. The agents were ushered through the shop and into a large, well-lit kitchen in the back, where they were warmly received by more *résistants,* among them a small, mild man introduced as Commandant Charles, who claimed to be in charge of local operations. Both groups had urgent questions: The inhabitants asked about the invasion of their country; the visitors wanted to know what was going on in the woods around the village. Corks popped, wine was poured, and the invasion was toasted, repeatedly.

One of the Sussac women, assuming correctly that the guests must be famished, said they must have something to eat. Before she could propose a menu, the agents requested, almost as one, eggs. The hosts protested that eggs were not nearly grand enough for an occasion such as this, but the visitors explained that they hadn't had fresh eggs in over a year, as rationing had limited them to the powdered variety. The villagers could scarcely believe that such a thing as powdered eggs existed. They made faces at the thought, and quickly served up plates of beautiful, fresh, sunny-side up eggs with bread and butter.

Sometime after 2:00 A.M. the agents were shown upstairs to rooms that had been prepared for them. Jean Claude, exhausted and relaxed with wine, fell into a deep sleep.

He was awakened about nine the next morning with a small tumbler of calvados. If that wasn't enough to make him realize he was back in France, he experienced a rush of nostalgia triggered by the coarseness of his linen bedsheets. When, as a boy, he visited his elderly aunt Katrinette on her farm, she always gave him her best sheets from her trousseau. They were family treasures—Katrinette had embroidered them by hand as a young woman, before she married—but they were so seldom used that they remained coarse almost to the point of scratchiness. The sheets he lay in that morning in Sussac, he thought, had to be from his hostess's trousseau.

Jean Claude joined the others downstairs for breakfast—more eggs. Members of the reception committee had brought in their suitcases and Jean Claude's radio, and were enjoying some of the real coffee the agents had brought.

Philippe and Jean Claude encoded a brief message to Baker Street announcing the team's safe arrival, and after breakfast the four Salesman agents, accompanied by Commandant Charles, set off to find a place to make their first transmission. Fortunately, the schedule did not call for the frequency of the lost crystal. They carried the radio to an isolated spot on a hill off a dirt road. Jean Claude tied a rock to the end of his antenna wire and threw it over a telegraph cable suspended from a pole, the only elevated structure around. Philippe, who wanted to make an impression on Commandant Charles, worried that the cable could cause interference. Jean Claude had no idea whether it would, but feigned confidence and crouched down to tune his set, as the prearranged hour for transmission had arrived.

He tapped out the Morse code message as the others watched.

He received no response.

He repeated the transmission.

No reply.

He sent it again.

The home station came in, loud and clear, signaling receipt of the message. Jean Claude breathed a sigh of relief, then adjusted his watch, realizing that in his eagerness to perform, he had begun his transmission a little early.

Operation Salesman II was under way.

PART

═ THREE ═

16

At the moment Jean Claude was tapping out his first coded message to London, a band of Resistance fighters in Tulle, a town forty-five miles to the south, was savoring an early taste of victory over the German occupiers. It quickly proved to be a cruel illusion.

Tulle was an industrial town that clung to the steep hills above the river Vézère, known for the manufacture of lace, munitions, and accordions. Local political sentiment was strongly Communist—not out of any special love for Moscow, but deriving from a homegrown, militant workers' movement that went back generations. The thick woods around Tulle were home to thousands of *maquisards* belonging to the *Francs-Tireurs et Partisans,* the armed wing of the French Communist Party (the name translates roughly as Partisan Sharpshooters). This band of FTP fighters was armed with Sten guns, Bren guns, grenades, and bazookas supplied by SOE. But they did not have agents sent from London to train them in weapons handling, organization, or tactics.

On the morning after D-Day, June 7, the *maquisards* determined to do their part in the liberation: They would storm the German garrison at Tulle and take over the town. The German forces consisted of several hundred elderly reservists, backed by secret police and a contingent of despised Vichyite Nazi sympathizers.

At 5:00 A.M., signaled by a bazooka blast, about a thousand FTP fighters emerged from the woods and began streaming into Tulle. They advanced street by street, house by house, the Germans returning fire from windows and rooftops. Both sides incurred casualties. By late morning the *maquisards* had taken over the city hall, the post office, and the train station. A group of Vichyites left the town that afternoon under a white flag, but the German troops, holed up in solid buildings with plenty of ammunition, showed no inclination to surrender. The guerrillas had neither air support nor artillery to dislodge them.

Night fell on an uneasy stalemate: the *maquisards* held most of the town, but the Germans still occupied two schools and Tulle's big munitions factory. Some of the guerrillas slipped back into the woods to rest; others collapsed with fatigue in houses in the town.

When fighting resumed in the morning, it had the flavor of a siege: The *maquisards* closed in on the German strongholds, and the Germans stayed put, firing back. In the afternoon the guerrillas worked their way close enough to one of the schools, the *École Normale,* to set it on fire. At about 4:00 P.M. a white flag was thrust out the door. About forty Germans came out with their hands over their heads and were led away by triumphant *maquisards.* By nightfall the guerrillas considered Tulle to be theirs. They looked after the wounded, carried away the dead, and made plans to roust the remaining Germans in the morning.

That's when the Waffen SS arrived.

At around 9:00 on the evening of June 8, tanks of the 2nd SS Panzer Division *Das Reich* roared into Tulle from three directions, accompanied by about five hundred soldiers. The *maquisards* immediately fled into the hills. The SS troops swept the streets, freed the besieged Germans, and set up a command post near the munitions factory.

The next morning, the German soldiers rounded up all the boys and men in Tulle between the ages of sixteen and sixty. They herded the hostages, about three thousand in all, into a big courtyard in front of the factory. They commandeered the town fire engine and sent it through the streets. A man on the fire engine rang its bell for attention and read a proclamation:

"Because of the indescribable murder of forty German soldiers by communist *maquisards,* the German authorities have decided that three Frenchmen will pay for each German killed, as an example to all France."[1]

The SS officers claimed to have found, early that morning, the bodies of forty Germans who had been taken prisoner and subsequently executed, their corpses horribly mutilated. The claim, never verified, has been dismissed by French historians as Nazi propaganda.

The SS men selected 120 men and boys from the crowd in the courtyard. In groups of 10 they were escorted to the avenue de la Gare, the main thoroughfare, where they were greeted by a ghastly sight: nooses dangled from lampposts, tree branches, and balconies.

The hangings began at around 4:00 in the afternoon and went on for three hours. Two ladders were used for each execution. A Frenchman was led up one. An SS man climbed the other, adjusted the noose around the victim's neck, and pushed him off. SS officers watched from a table outside the Café Tivoli, drinking wine and listening to music from a gramophone.

At around 7:00 in the evening, with 99 corpses suspended along the avenue, the killings were halted. It isn't clear why the Germans didn't murder all of the condemned. Another 149 men were transported to Dachau, where 101 of them lost their lives.

The commander for this operation was an SS intelligence officer, *Sturmbannführer* (Major) Aurel Kowatsch. Just before the hangings began, he received a last-minute plea from the prefect of Tulle to carry out reprisals in some other way. He replied, "We have developed on the Russian front the practice of hanging. We have hanged more than one hundred thousand in Kharkov and in Kiev. This is nothing to us."

This sketch, the only known visual record of the massacre at
Tulle on June 9, 1944, was made by a Nazi officer present. At least
thirty bodies can be seen hanging from lampposts and balconies.

THE *STURMBANNFÜHRER* DID not exaggerate. By the time they reached that part of France, the troops of the 2nd SS Panzer Division were old hands at murdering noncombatants. There is no doubt that the Waffen SS was among the most effective fighting forces the world has ever seen. It was also found, at the postwar International Military Tribunal at Nuremberg, to be a criminal organization.

The SS did not have its roots in the regular military. It originated before the war as a personal security service for Hitler—SS stands for *Schutzstaffel,* or "protection squadron." (*Waffen* in this context simply means "armed.") Under the direction of Heinrich Himmler, it grew into a vast cult of violence that undertook the worst of the Nazi atrocities, including the construction and operation of death camps. The SS had its own schools, publications, rituals, and institutions—even a monumental castle in Westphalia. Its soldiers were indoctrinated to believe in their own "Nordic" racial superiority, and to treat the enemy as vermin. They were the fruit of Hitler's promise to turn Germany's young Nazis into "magnificent beasts of prey."

The most savage killing grounds in Europe were in the east, and it was there that the 2nd SS Panzer Division served before coming to France. The scale of the brutality there was almost unimaginable, as it was intended to be: In what they called the "Hunger Plan," Nazi leaders aimed to win a quick summertime victory over the Red Army, and then starve 30 million Soviets to death. The plan envisioned the "extinction of industry as well as a great part of the population," leaving a vast, depopulated eastern prairie ready for German agrarian colonization. Before the project was defeated by the Red Army and the Russian winter of 1941–42—"General Winter," as rueful Germans called it—millions of Soviet civilians and soldiers lost their lives.

The Germans wiped out many hundreds of villages during their advance and retreat through the Soviet Union. Civilian massacres large and small were routine. Jews and others considered "subhuman" were regularly rounded up to be hanged, shot, buried alive, or asphyxiated in vans that had their exhaust fumes piped into sealed passenger compartments—a Soviet invention, but one that was adopted enthusiastically by the Nazis.

The 2nd SS Panzer Division *Das Reich,* regarded as the "jewel" of Hitler's thirty-eight Waffen SS divisions, campaigned across the eastern front. It fought in the major battles of Moscow, Kharkov, and Kursk. In Lahoysk, a city in what is now Belarus, it took part in the murder of 920 Jews.

By October 1943 the division was exhausted. It had won more Iron Crosses than any other Panzer division, but it had lost 70 percent of its men. It was ordered by Himmler to withdraw and regroup.

The *Das Reich* division rolled westward, leaving a trail of murdered civilians in Czechoslovakia and Belgium before coming to a halt in Montauban, near Toulouse, in south-central France. There it spent the winter of 1943–44, refitting and rebuilding its ranks. By D-Day it was back at full strength, with fifteen thousand infantrymen, more than two hundred Panzer and Tiger tanks, and extensive armored artillery. Commanded by *Brigadeführer* (Brigadier General) Heinz Lammerding, the division was held in central France with the expectation that it would rush north to the English Channel, or south to the Mediterranean, depending on where the Allied invaders came ashore.

Resistance groups in the countryside around Montauban harried the Germans that winter and spring. SOE's F Section had at least three circuits—code-named Wheelwright, Clergyman, and Footman—operating in the region. On May 2, *Das Reich* tanks on a training exercise were fired upon. In retribution, German soldiers murdered sixteen civilians in the village of Montpezat-de-Quercy, including a two-year-old girl they burned to death. Over the next nine days, in response to guerrilla attacks and acts of sabotage, they burned and looted scores of houses and barns to the northwest of Montauban; more than fifty civilians were arrested and deported to Germany. On May 12, after finding a Resistance arms cache in Figeac, *Das Reich* soldiers rounded up more than eight hundred townspeople. Some were tortured, some were shot, and 540 were sent to the concentration camps at Dachau and Neuengamme.

When D-Day finally arrived, the *Das Reich* division was ordered to move north to the Normandy beaches. On the way, it was instructed to crush the French Resistance. "For every German wounded or killed," Lammerding told his men, "we will kill ten terrorists." On June 8, the division set out on the N20 highway toward Limoges, 160 miles to the north.

The simple fact that *Das Reich* traveled by road represented a victory for the Resistance. Tanks were customarily moved between battlegrounds by rail or by flatbed truck; they were chronically prone to break down if they had to drive long distances on their own treads. But *maquisards* led by SOE officers blew up the north-south rail lines in the region, and kept blowing them up as fast as the Germans could repair them.

Climbing into the beautiful hill country of the Lot region, chewing up the highway as it went, *Das Reich* split into three parallel columns. A little band of *maquisards* in the hamlet of Groslejac opened fire with bolt-action rifles as one of the columns passed through; the Germans machine-gunned them, killing them all, along with five civilians. At Carsac, the Germans fired on villagers, killing thirteen. When they reached Rouffillac, the SS men found the road barricaded. They swept the roadblock aside, killing one *maquisard* and fifteen civilians. As dusk fell, the sky was lit with flames from houses and barns torched by the Germans. That night the German tanks began arriving in Limoges—though not the *Aufklärungsabteilung,* or reconnaissance battalion. That was the unit sent to Tulle.

The next day, June 9, the Germans continued their campaign against the guerrillas. *Maquisards* attacked the town of Argenton-sur-Creuse, to the east of Limoges. The 3rd Battalion of *Das Reich* took the town back, killing fifty-four people, including boys and women.

The commander of that battalion was one of the most highly decorated men in the Third Reich, *Sturmbannführer* Helmut Kämpfe. A thirty-four-year-old who had been a printer before the war, Kämpfe was wounded ten times in combat and was awarded the Knight's Cross of the Iron Cross, the Reich's highest honor. He was friendly with Hitler and well regarded by his men.

As evening fell, Kämpfe headed back toward Limoges, alone, driving a car on the N141 road. With about fifteen miles to go, he was ambushed and surrounded by a group of FTP *maquisards*. The Resistance fighters spirited Kämpfe away to their encampment in the woods, leaving his car in the road with its doors open and its engine running. They quickly realized what a prize they had—Kämpfe was, in fact, the highest-ranking German officer captured by the Resistance during the war.

17

Around the time Kämpfe was ambushed, Jean Claude and Violette, back in Sussac, were taking an after-dinner stroll along a country lane outside the town. Violette pushed an old but serviceable bicycle. It was the first time they had been alone together.

They had dined, fairly well, in the big kitchen behind the dry-goods store. It had a large table, mismatched wooden chairs, and a plank for a bar, and it served as a sort of informal village café. In this rural part of France, the Limousin region, the privations of wartime rationing were not as severe as in cities. Caffeine and cigarettes were in short supply, to be sure; people in Sussac made "coffee" from roasted barley and ground acorns, and tea from linden flowers, and they rolled up a mixture of chopped grass and leaves for their smokes. But in addition to the beef cattle for which the Limousin is famous, the farming communities there had fresh vegetables, mushrooms, ducks, lamb, fish, and all the game they could hunt. They made their own wine and cheese. At the communal oven they still made crusty white bread, not the darker kind that most of the country had in wartime. One memorable night later in the Salesman II mission, the backroom café served roast suckling pig for dinner.

As they walked, Jean Claude and Violette talked about life, and the nature of risk, and the events of their mission so far. Jean Claude was a bit smitten, and he could recall the conversation clearly many decades later.

It had been a busy forty-eight hours. The Salesman agents had wasted no time getting to work after making contact with London that first morning in the presence of Commandant Charles. Bob spent much of the day sorting plastic explosives, detonators, and timers, and finding places around Sussac to hide them. To make an immediate impression on the *maquisards,* he led two volunteers on a sabotage raid that very evening. They slipped through dark woods to a railroad track—a target chosen from a list provided by Baker Street—and Bob showed the men how to derail a train. He removed four lag screws from the wooden tie where two sections of track met. He used a pry bar to separate the track sections by about four inches, holding them apart with one of the lag screws. He scooped out a few handfuls of gravel, laid down a plastic charge, inserted a blasting cap, and ran wire to the nuts on the base of a magneto blasting detonator. When a train arrived he raised the detonator handle, twisted it three times, and shoved it rapidly down, creating an electrical charge that triggered a blast. The train jumped the track, and the men fled amid machine-gun fire. Bob was wounded very slightly in the arm.

Philippe, meanwhile, took the first steps toward recruiting an army. There was no time to lose—the false starts had delayed the Salesman mission by three days, and reports from the invasion beaches were mixed at best. It would be a disaster if the *Das Reich* division was permitted to pass through the Limousin unopposed.

Thousands of potential guerrillas were hiding in the woods, but insofar as they were organized at all, they belonged to fractious groups with divergent agendas and allegiances. The FTP, aligned with the French Communist Party, was suspicious of the Allies because it feared they would suppress Communism after the war. Right-wing nationalists didn't want to fight alongside, and thus legitimate, the

Communists. Socialists and anarchists had agendas of their own. Thousands of *maquisards* were antifascist Spanish refugees, defeated veterans of the Spanish Civil War.

Charles de Gaulle, from his exile in London, had tried to unite these groups under the leadership of the Resistance hero Jean Moulin. That effort collapsed after Moulin was captured in 1943 and tortured to death by Klaus Barbie, the "Butcher of Lyon." De Gaulle and SOE coordinated some of their Resistance activities, but there was little love lost between them. De Gaulle considered SOE to be meddling in French affairs; Baker Street regarded de Gaulle as a blowhard with dangerously childlike notions of security.

Philippe's job was to persuade the factions in his part of the Limousin—principally the Haute-Vienne, Corrèze, Creuse, Charente, and Indre departments—to set aside their differences and fight, under his command, against their common enemy. His starting point, the key contact SOE had sent him to meet, was Commandant Charles.

On that first day in Sussac, Charles led Philippe to an abandoned rock hut outside of town, a disused water mill with a stream running through it, and proposed it as a spot to hide the team's radio. Philippe was pleased. He thought that he and Jean Claude could live there together for the duration of the mission. Charles arranged for basic furnishings for two to be delivered.

When the conversation turned to fighting, though, Philippe began to have doubts. It was clear that Commandant Charles had been in radio contact with Baker Street, and that Baker Street had dropped him supplies. But he seemed to have scant useful information, few men at his command, and little inclination to take up arms.

By the second day, after many hours of talks, Philippe came to the alarming conclusion that Commandant Charles was a fraud. A dancehall saxophone player in civilian life, he had served in the French army as a private but had never seen combat. Philippe described the situation this way, in a report months later to Baker Street:

"When I left London I was given to understand that I would find on arrival a very well organized Maquis, strictly devoid of any political intrigues, which would constitute a very good basis for extending a circuit throughout the area. On arrival I did find a Maquis, which was roughly 600 strong, plus 200 gendarmes who joined up on D-Day; but these men were strictly not trained, and commanded by the most incapable people I have ever met."

Exploring the lanes around Sussac, Jean Claude and Violette found themselves at the bottom of a long hill. Dusk was approaching, and Jean Claude wanted to show Violette the old mill that was to be his new home. They came across a horse-drawn cart that was heading back up the hill, in the direction of the mill, and hitched a ride. They loaded Violette's bicycle onto the cart and sat together. Violette expressed the highest regard for Philippe, so much so that Jean Claude wondered if she was trying to give him confidence in their leader. With conviction, but without bravado, she said she shared Philippe's view that a person must take chances in life—that life itself may be thought of as a chance.

Violette told Jean Claude that she would be doing some traveling the next morning. Philippe had swiftly concluded that to get around the Commandant Charles problem he must make contact with SOE circuits already operating in territory nearby, and find out what they knew about the *maquis*. He planned to send Violette to contact a circuit about one hundred miles to the southwest.

When they reached the mill it was almost dark. They returned to town and parted ways. Jean Claude happily set up his radio, encoded a long message from Philippe to Baker Street, and settled in to listen to the Broadcast.

Each evening the BBC, at the conclusion of its French-language newscast, sounded the opening notes of Beethoven's Fifth Symphony, played on timpani. The meaning was clear to those in the know: The rhythm of the musical phrase—dot dot dot dash—made the letter V, signifying victory, in Morse code. Then an announcer said, *"Et voici maintenant quelques messages personnels"* ("And now here are some personal messages"). At that prompt, Resistance members all over France stopped what they were doing to listen to strings of odd, unconnected sentences, like "The dice are on the carpet," or "There is a fire at the insurance agency." They seemed to be random nonsense, but they were coded communications from London. The first one Jean Claude heard was *"Josephine a des fesses d'ébène,"* or "Josephine has ebony buttocks." He never found out what it meant, and he never forgot it.

The Broadcast was the most public stratagem devised by SOE, and among the most brilliant. It eliminated the need for radio operators to switch on their sets to receive messages from the home station. It boosted French morale and infuriated the Germans, who knew that instructions to insurgents were being sent over some of the world's most powerful transmitters and could do nothing about it. Agents used the Broadcast to establish their bona fides with recruits. If, say, a group of *maquisards* doubted a stranger's claim that he had been sent by London to arm and lead them—suspecting, perhaps, that he was a collaborator sent to entrap them—the agent could ask them to volunteer a phrase, and then have it broadcast by the BBC.

Most often, the messages were coded notifications of where and when parachute drops were to be made. If more than one drop was planned, the phrase "we repeat" would indicate the number. Thus, "Remember the great raspberries in mother's garden, we repeat two times, remember the great raspberries in mother's garden," signified two drops on a particular zone to occur the following night, each drop being a planeload.

The Broadcast was made twice a day, orally after the French newscast in the early evening, and again in Morse code, with additional specific messages, starting around 9:00 P.M. Jean Claude's task was to listen to the Morse Broadcast and copy and decode any messages for Philippe.

So began a period of sleep-deprived, harried, isolated labor for Jean Claude. Coding and decoding took up much of his time, often late into the night. In addition to the Broadcast, each day, by prearrangement with Baker Street, Jean Claude had a scheduled time for sending and receiving messages over his wireless set. The time for each schedule varied daily, as did the call signs and the frequency for the transmission. Even if he had nothing to send he had to listen, in case Baker Street tried to make contact. There were also several alternative schedules each day, to be used if there was an emergency, if the original schedule was unusable due to static, or if the volume of messages was too large to send all at once.

Philippe insisted that Jean Claude was to hide and stay put. As the link with London, he was too valuable to send out on operations.

Jean Claude made clear to Philippe that on the contrary, he wanted to do his part as a trained SOE agent and take the fight to the enemy.

He didn't have to wait long.

18

German soldiers came across *Sturmbannführer* Kämpfe's abandoned car on the evening of June 9, about the time Jean Claude was listening to the Broadcast. Its front wheels were nosed off the road onto the grassy verge. A Schmeisser machine pistol without a clip lay on the ground. There was no blood or other sign of struggle.

When word of Kämpfe's disappearance reached the *Das Reich* commanders at their billet in Limoges, they reacted with fury. They ordered roadblocks to be set up, and sent search parties to scour the countryside around the abandoned car throughout the night. SS soldiers stopped two farmers, questioned them, found that they had no information, shot them, and left their bodies in a roadside ditch.

Early the next morning, Saturday, June 10, two French collaborators approached Adolf Diekmann, commander of the 1st Battalion of the 4th Panzer Grenadier Regiment, with a rumor. Diekmann held the same rank as Kämpfe, *Sturmbannführer,* and was his close friend. The collaborators were members of the *Milice,* the French paramilitary force organized by the Vichy government to fight the Resistance. The *Milice* was generally considered more dangerous than the Gestapo, as its members had a similar enthusiasm for torture but were natives with local knowledge.

The two *miliciens* told Diekmann that they had heard that Kämpfe was being held by a band of *maquisards* near a village called Oradour-sur-Vayres, twenty-five miles to the west. The *maquisards,* they said, planned to execute him and burn his body publicly.

Diekmann roared out of Limoges with two half-tracks, eight trucks, and 120 SS soldiers, leading the way in a commandeered Citroën 2CV. The convoy drove to Oradour-sur-Glane, fourteen miles to the north-west. It isn't clear why they went to the wrong village; it might have been simple confusion about the name. In any case, there is no evidence that Kämpfe was held by *maquisards* associated with either Oradour.

Oradour-sur-Glane was a pleasant little market town nestled among farms in the Haute-Vienne. Ordinarily it was home to about 330 people, but on this sunny Saturday its population was twice that, swollen by refugees—some Spaniards, some Jews, some city dwellers seeking a haven from bombers—and by local farmers making a weekend visit to buy supplies and collect their tobacco ration. Many were just finishing lunch when the Germans arrived, a little after 2:00 P.M.

Oradour-sur-Glane was such a placid backwater that even in 1944 it had a town crier. Diekmann gave orders for him to proceed through the streets, beating his drum, and summon everyone to the Champ de Foire, a little fairground at the center of the village, to have their identity papers checked. A few people fled, but nearly all complied. They had done nothing wrong, after all, and the village had no strategic value for the Germans.

The SS soldiers trained MG 42s on the crowd—machine guns with such a high rate of fire that they were nicknamed "Hitler's buzz saw," as the ear could not distinguish individual shots when they were fired. The soldiers separated the men from the women and children. They led the 197 men away and locked them into six barns at the edge of town. Then they locked the others—240 women and 205 children—in the village church.

The SS soldiers machine-gunned the men in the barns, aiming low, at their legs. Once the victims were unable to move, the soldiers piled straw and brush on top of them and burned the barns to the ground.

Then a group of soldiers carried a heavy box into the church and set it down near the altar. They lit a fuse attached to it. Thick black smoke poured out, but whatever was in the box didn't detonate completely. The women and children panicked and tried to flee through doors and windows. The soldiers machine-gunned them and threw incendiary grenades into the church. Then they heaped straw and wooden furniture onto the piles of dead and wounded, and set it alight. The church's roof beams caught fire and collapsed.

The Germans killed 642 civilians that afternoon. Six men survived the slaughter in the barns, saved by corpses that fell on top of them. Only one woman survived, a forty-seven-year-old named Marguerite Rouffanche. She jumped out of the church by a sacristy window and landed nine feet down. Looking up, she saw a woman at the window holding out a baby to her. A burst of machine-gun fire killed the baby and the woman at the window, and wounded Rouffanche. She crawled to a field nearby, dug a shallow trench with her hands in soft, newly tilled soil between pea plants, covered herself with dirt, and hid, bleeding, for twenty-four hours. That night the Germans looted and torched the village.

The atrocity at Oradour was the worst massacre of innocents on French soil in World War II. A few days afterward, Jean Claude went to the village and surveyed the ruins. He took photographs of charred corpses left in heaps. He loaned the photos to Bob Maloubier's brother, a journalist, after the liberation of Paris. Published in a Parisian newspaper in late September 1944, they were among the first images providing evidence of the crime.

Jean Claude could barely bring himself to speak of Oradour-sur-Glane for the rest of his life. Whenever he was asked about the events of that day, he calmly but firmly changed the subject.

Oradour-sur-Glane after the massacre, photographed by
Jean Claude sometime between June 14 and June 21, 1944,
when a brief burial ceremony was allowed by the Nazis.

19

Had Philippe known that *Das Reich* troops were frantically scouring the countryside in search of *Sturmbannführer* Kämpfe on the day of the Oradour massacre, he would undoubtedly have made different tactical choices. As it was, he had scant local intelligence, an urgent need for recruits, and a difficult decision to make: Should he proceed with discretion, or with speed?

Philippe determined that his best chance of locating effective Resistance fighters would be to make contact with a nearby SOE circuit code-named Digger. Its agents had been operating in the Corrèze department for months; they had already armed more than four thousand *maquisards* and presumably they knew the lay of the land. The Digger agents operated from a safe house in a village called Brive-la-Gaillarde, fifty miles to the south.

The prudent course for Philippe would be to send his courier by bicycle. Violette was accustomed to long-distance cycling, and a woman traveling alone, unarmed, wouldn't be likely to arouse suspicion. Even if she were stopped at a checkpoint she could probably bluff her way through, as she had a complete set of expertly forged papers identifying her as a Mme. Villeret, the widow of an antique dealer from Nantes.

One of the *maquisards* in Sussac, a man named Jacques Dufour, had an alternative suggestion. He told Philippe that he knew where to find some of the Resistance groups in the Corrèze. He also had a car. He volunteered to drive Violette and make introductions, starting with a group south of Arnac-Pompadour, a little more than halfway to the Digger safe house. He would drop her off, and then Violette could move around the region on her bike, making contact with more bands of fighters.

Traveling by automobile would automatically arouse suspicion—the Nazis had banned car travel by French civilians after D-Day—but it would be far quicker. Dufour knew the back roads intimately, and they would have only one major highway to cross, the A20.

Philippe decided to take the chance.

Violette's bicycle was lashed to the side of Dufour's big black Citroën Traction Avant. She asked Philippe for a Sten gun, and he gave her one, with extra clips. Dufour had a Marlin submachine gun, an American weapon that was slightly more accurate than the Sten.

Dufour and Violette drove out of Sussac at 9:30 on the morning of June 10. They stopped at a village called La Croisille-sur-Briance and picked up a friend of Dufour, Jean Bariaud, who was to accompany him on the return trip. They drove on for twelve miles. Dufour decided to cross the A20 highway where it passed by Salon-la-Tour, his hometown.

Coming around a bend in the road just outside Salon-la-Tour, they saw a German roadblock fifty yards ahead. It was a squad of *Das Reich* soldiers searching for Major Kämpfe. There was no question of trying to bluff their way through. Dufour braked to a halt short of the roadblock, and they stepped out of the car.

Bariaud, who was unarmed, sprinted away. The Germans opened fire. Violette and Dufour ran crouching along a ditch and vaulted a fence into a farmyard, carrying their weapons. They ran through a neighboring farmyard, past a hedge, down a meadow, and across a stream at its far end.

SS soldiers charged after them. When the pursuers came to the second farm they asked the farmer which way they had gone. He pointed the soldiers in the wrong direction, and Violette and Dufour gained some ground.

They raced uphill through a broad cornfield toward a dirt road. On the far side of the road were some woods. If they could reach the trees they might escape.

Soldiers spotted them running through the field and opened fire with machine guns. A bullet grazed Violette's left arm. She and Dufour ran a zigzag pattern through the cornstalks, each pausing to return the Germans' fire and provide cover for the other. A pair of *Das Reich* armored cars began moving along the dirt road between the top of the cornfield and the woods, to block their escape route.

Before they could reach the safety of the trees, Violette twisted an ankle and fell. Dufour tried to pick her up and carry her, but she pushed him away, insisting that he keep running and save himself. She crawled to an apple tree, hauled herself upright, clamped a fresh magazine into her Sten, and opened fire. Dufour turned and sprinted on toward the tree line.

The armored cars roared up the road, heading for the same spot as Dufour. Scores of German soldiers poured into the cornfield, converging on Violette's position. Some of them fell, either wounded or killed. She kept firing.

Dufour lost his footrace with the armored cars. He had to veer off before he reached the trees. Near the top of the field was a small farmhouse he knew well—it was owned by the Montintin family, and he had gone to school with the farmer's two daughters. Dufour reached the farmyard with just enough time to hide under a small haystack. His foot stuck out, and one of the daughters, Suzanne, sat on it.

Violette kept the German soldiers at bay for the better part of half an hour, firing when she saw movement in the cornstalks. But she couldn't run on her bad ankle, and the gunfight's conclusion was foregone. She emptied the last of her magazines, and her Sten fell silent. The SS men cautiously surrounded her. She was exhausted and bleeding. A young officer offered her a cigarette. She refused it. The officer told her in broken French that she was the bravest woman he had ever met. She spat in his face.

The soldiers took her for questioning to the very farmyard where Dufour was hiding. Under his haystack he heard the *Das Reich* troopers demanding where he had gone. Violette, laughing, replied: "You can run after him, he is far away by now."

The soldiers put Violette into one of the armored cars and drove her to Limoges, thirty miles to the north. There, at the Gestapo headquarters, they handed her over for interrogation to *Sturmbannführer* Aurel Kowatsch, the man who had overseen the hangings at Tulle the day before.

20

Jean Claude was working at a wooden table in the old millhouse the next afternoon, encoding messages about potential drop zones and supplies, when Philippe burst in and asked him how quickly they could make their next contact with Baker Street.

Jean Claude had spent the previous day transforming the rock hut into what was surely one of the world's most primitive radio stations. The tiny house had a single main room and a pair of alcoves, one with a window and the other with a pump and a stone sink. The floor was dirt, and a stream ran down the middle of it, entering and exiting through rough openings in the walls. An outhouse stood in the bushes a short distance away.

A single bare lightbulb hung from the hut's ceiling, pulsing occasionally due to the spotty power supply. Jean Claude got lucky and found a double socket at the dry-goods store in Sussac, so he could use the light and his radio at the same time. It would be another couple of weeks before he obtained a generator and connected it to the water-wheel driven by the stream.

Some of Commandant Charles's men had lugged in two bedsteads with sagging springs, two old mattresses, blankets and pillows, and a table and two chairs. Jean Claude swept out the cobwebs and set up the main room as his bedroom and work space. He didn't have to make room for Philippe, as it turned out; Philippe's duties kept him so busy, especially after nightfall, that he never moved in as intended.

Now, though, Philippe stood beneath the sagging roof beams and delivered his terrible news: Violette had been taken prisoner. Philippe had received a report from Bariaud, the passenger who had fled the roadblock. He had made his way home to La Croisille and sent word on to Sussac. Bariaud said that Dufour had probably been captured as well.

Jean Claude switched on his wireless set, and a flurry of radio traffic with London ensued. The static was terrible that day, necessitating many repetitions and changes of frequency. Each repetition raised the risk of detection. Jean Claude, shocked and apprehensive, was surprised at Philippe's concise, dispassionate communications. He was even more surprised several months later when he discovered that Philippe and Violette were old friends. They had told him nothing about the first Operation Salesman, or about the perils they had faced in Rouen and Le Havre.

Two days later, on June 13, Jacques Dufour reappeared in Sussac. He had not been captured after all. He had stayed under his haystack until the Germans gave up their search for him, and then had been hidden on the farm by the Montintin family.

By then Philippe had made contact with members of the Resistance in Limoges. They told him that one of Violette's jailers was asking for money "to help look after her."

Over the next week or so Philippe used his contacts in the city to find out all he could about the conditions of Violette's captivity. He made payments to the jailer, who reported that she was doing as well as could be expected. He learned that each day Violette was walked from the Limoges prison to the Gestapo headquarters, some two hundred yards away, and back. She limped badly. She was not shackled, but she was escorted by a pair of German guards, one on either side.

Phillippe and Bob made a plan to snatch her. One of the Limoges Resistance men had a car they could use. Bob had a brace of Welrod pistols. They decided that Bob would be driven to a point between the prison and the Gestapo headquarters. When Violette limped by, Bob would step out of the car and shoot her guards. Violette and Bob would get into the car and be driven out of town to safety. If they came to a checkpoint they would simply blast their way through with Sten guns.

Before they could take action, though, they got more dreadful news: the Germans had taken Violette away. They didn't know where. But they discovered that she had been held in Limoges for no more than a few days; the jailer had been stringing them along for the money. They never saw Violette again.

Evidently Violette did not give up her comrades when she was interrogated by *Sturmbannführer* Kowatsch in Limoges. She gave her name as Vicky Taylor, which was a cover that had been prepared for her to use if she should need to escape to England via Spain. (The Hungarian word for "tailor" is *szabo*.) But her captors were not fooled. They moved her to the notorious Fresnes Prison on the outskirts of Paris, and from there they took her to 84 avenue Foch, the headquarters of the *Sicherheitsdienst,* the intelligence service of the SS. The avenue Foch is one of the most elegant boulevards in Paris, but during the war it was known as "the street of horrors." Number 84 was where the SS interrogated SOE agents captured in France.

21

Jean Claude was deeply shaken by Violette's loss, and depressed at the thought that Operation Salesman II was looking wobbly after just a few days. Neither he nor the others had any time to grieve for Violette, however. Her disappearance made them even busier than they were already, as they had to divide up her duties—chiefly the scouting of drop zones and the recruiting of reception committees—among themselves.

The feckless Commandant Charles notwithstanding, French men and women in the Limousin region had been resisting the German occupation vigorously for some time. Limoges, the capital city, was under the tight control of the Nazis, to be sure. But the countryside all around it was a congenial place to be a guerrilla. Situated on the northwest edge of the Massif Central, the rugged uplands of central France, the Limousin was, and is, among the wildest and least populous areas of the country—part of the broad swath that is sometimes called "empty France." Steep canyons and gorges cut through plateaus and rolling hills; pastures are bordered by dense, expansive forestland. In 1944 there were few paved roads. People generally moved about via extensive, labyrinthine networks of narrow cantonal pathways and trails. A traveler on one of these rural dirt roads might find that it dead-ended at a high, remote pasture, or at a cliff's edge. Local knowledge was important.

Many major rail routes traversed the countryside connecting distant large cities. The tracks crossed rivers and crevasses over stone viaducts and timber trestles. Often they wound along river gorges or through narrow rail cuts with high banks on either side.

Towns and villages were small and isolated. The residents were independent minded and accustomed to making their own way. Not surprisingly, they had little regard for the directives of the central government—even when the government was authentically French, and most assuredly when it was not. Since the start of the occupation, bands of armed men had periodically harassed German patrols that dared to leave the safety of Limoges.

They were not, however, armed with much besides hunting rifles, or organized in any uniform way. De Gaulle had made another attempt, shortly before the invasion, to unite the Resistance factions, calling for them to fight together under the rubric of the *Forces Françaises de l'Intérieur,* or French Forces of the Interior. In the long run this was a success: When the liberators finally rolled into Paris later that summer, many guerrillas wore the blue, white, and red armband of the FFI. But in the weeks following D-Day, the *maquisards* of the Limousin— Gaullists, Communists, Socialists, and others—remained suspicious of one another's political motives. They might have had a common enemy, but what vision of postwar France were they fighting for?

Philippe did find small bands of *maquisards* near other villages— Pressac and Blond to the northwest, and Gramont to the south—who were willing to set aside politics and take up the arms he could summon from the sky. He set them to work attacking railways, bridges, and power lines. It was a start, but the assaults were pinpricks, relatively speaking—if Operation Salesman was to succeed, Philippe was going to need a lot more men in a hurry. Commandant Charles was no help, and soon became a hindrance. He wanted the matériel that

London could provide, but he hesitated to send his men into harm's way. Philippe gave him an ultimatum: Charles must submit to his orders or there would be no supplies. Charles took it badly. Discussions grew tense, then hostile. The Salesman agents began to fear that Charles might go so far as to take Jean Claude hostage, to break contact with London.

Philippe sent out feelers to collect intelligence about other *maquis* groups in the Limousin. He began to hear rumors about a mysterious figure said to command a large force of fighters hidden deep in the countryside. Some called him the *Préfet du Maquis* (the Prefect of the Maquis). Others called him the *Préfet Rouge* (the "Red Prefect"), or simply *Lo Grand* (the "Great One," in Limousin dialect). Philippe couldn't determine whether this was a real man or a wishful apparition, the product of the collective imagination of a community living under occupation.

Bob, in those first few days, had a far more straightforward job. In the daylight hours he trained small groups of recruits in the handling of explosives, detonators, timers, Sten guns, Bren guns, grenades, and bazookas. When darkness fell he led them on raids, sometimes two or three in a single night. He typically stole a few hours of sleep around sunrise. In short order Bob's commandos cut the north-south railway lines at Brive, Tulle, and Uzerche.

Jean Claude, meanwhile, spent long hours at the table in his rock hut, coding and decoding messages, communicating in Morse with Baker Street, and listening to the Broadcast. With Violette gone, though, Philippe needed someone to help with drop zone work. He relaxed his rule against putting Jean Claude in danger, and began sending him out to scout DZs and organize reception committees when his radio schedules permitted.

Jean Claude found DZ duty to be a thoroughly enjoyable way to wage war. The work usually began at around 11:00 P.M., and of course it was always on a moonlit night in clement weather. Jean Claude would make his way to a designated field with a group of locals, who usually brought wagons and carts drawn by draft animals. In the quiet, under the stars, they would set up signal lights or fires in an inverted L pattern and settle down to wait. The mood would shift to anticipation, then excitement, as the first distant drone of an airplane's big radial engines was heard.

As the plane came closer, the recognition signal—the Morse letter code—was flashed in the direction of the sound; the airplanes never showed any lights. Then it could be a hit-or-miss event. Sometimes a plane had to circle to come at the DZ from the right direction. Occasionally, to Jean Claude's great disappointment, a plane would keep right on going, either because it had missed the signal or because it was bound for another circuit. But if it all went as hoped, the plane would come in low with a roar and a swish of disturbed air and release its containers, which quickly floated to earth underneath their parachutes. The sound of the plane would diminish as it turned to head for home, or to make another pass.

Then the real work began. Summer nights were short and the moon was the reception committee's primary source of light. The canisters had to be located, collected, loaded onto wagons, and taken away before daybreak, as dawn brought the possibility of German or Vichy patrols and ID checks. The drops were not always accurate—canisters might land hundreds of yards, even miles, away from the DZ, or in nearby trees. Jean Claude found that English bomber crews were much better than Americans at hitting their targets. On one memorable night, a delivery containing several hundred thousand francs landed in the courtyard of a police station.

By far the most important duty was keeping track of the containers. There might be as many as a dozen per drop, each a cylindrical tube about thirty inches in diameter and about six feet long, weighing from 150 to 200 pounds, with handles on the sides. Some could be broken down into three sections, which made them easier to move. Jean

Claude was grateful for the assistance of the gendarmes who had joined up after D-Day, who proved reliable at collecting and delivering everything to the Salesman team in Sussac without pilferage.

Once everything had been removed from the DZ, farmers would drive their cows or sheep onto the matted grass left behind. By dawn the grazing animals would have erased most signs of the evening's activities.

22

G eorges Guingouin had been living in the woods for a long time. His thick glasses and flat feet gave him a decidedly nonmilitary air, but he called himself a colonel, and he had taken up guerrilla warfare in the Limousin long before the Nazis ordered the *Service du Travail Obligatoire,* the compulsory work decree that drove so many Frenchmen into the Resistance in 1943. Guingouin sometimes called himself "the first *maquisard* in France."

Guingouin was a Limousin native, born in Magnac-Laval, a village in the Haute-Vienne, in 1913. His father was killed fighting the Germans on the western front in World War I when Georges was just a year old, and he was raised by his mother, a teacher at an elementary school. He became a teacher himself in the 1930s, and also a member of the French Communist Party (PCF). This was not by any means a fringe affiliation at the time. Communism was not imported wholesale into France, but rather was grafted onto the living stem of a militant, antifascist, trade-union movement. The first French confederation of workers, the *Confédération Générale du Travail,* was created in Limoges in 1895, and was dominated by the PCF right up to the mid-1990s. In 1936, when Leon Blum became the country's first Socialist prime minister, his Popular Front government included 72 PCF representatives in Parliament (out of 608 seats). Guingouin became the secretary of the Communist Party of the small commune of Eymoutiers.

Conscripted into the French army when the war began, Guingouin was wounded above his left eye in June 1940 and taken to the military hospital at Moulins-sur-Allier. When that city came under German attack, he left his hospital bed to help with its defense. Afterward, discharged from the army, Guingouin made his way back to the Haute-Vienne and resumed teaching, at a school in Saint-Gilles-les-Forêts.

Guingouin was a doctrinaire Communist and a loyal PCF member, but he was no apparatchik. He was above all a principled, independent-minded militant. And so, when the Nazi occupation took hold of France, Guingouin found himself at odds with both the Vichy collaborators on the right, and the PCF on the left. The Vichy regime purged Communists from government jobs, and Guingouin was fired from his teaching position. Because the Hitler-Stalin pact was in effect at that early stage of the war, the PCF took a neutral stance vis-à-vis the German invaders; it instructed party members not to take sides in the "imperialist" war. Guingouin thought that was nonsense. He wrote and circulated a manifesto denouncing the Nazi occupation.

Then, in February 1941, he vanished into the forest outside Châteauneuf-la-Forêt to live as an outlaw.

Guingouin was joined by a handful of like-minded militants, and before long they had a substantial, well-hidden encampment about five miles from Sussac. At first they focused on propaganda. Paper was hard to come by, and they had to make ink by mixing soot into linseed oil, but they produced pamphlets urging resistance, and distributed them to farmers on market days.

Their numbers grew, albeit slowly at first. They engaged in small acts of sabotage, such as blowing up a baler to keep hay and wheat out of the hands of the occupiers. They destroyed the boilers at a rubber factory near Limoges. They cut a railway line between Limoges and Ussel. They discovered that a subterranean cable linking a Bordeaux submarine base with Berlin ran by Limoges, and they severed it.

In 1943 their numbers swelled after the German imposition of forced labor. Guingouin grew so bold as to assert his own administrative authority in the region, defying the Vichy government. He disliked the price gouging that went on in the black market. He set fixed prices for agricultural goods and posted them in villages.

He signed the documents: "Le Préfet du Maquis."

By the time the Salesman team made contact with him in their second week in France, Guingouin had more than three thousand men under his authority. It was by far the largest *maquis* group in the region. Philippe knew at once that Guingouin's army of outlaws would be the key to Operation Salesman's success, and he proposed to provide them with weapons if Guingouin would put them under his command.

Guingouin would have none of it. In his mind the Salesman agents represented the Allies, whom he distrusted fundamentally: He feared that they would suppress Communism after the war. He had no love for de Gaulle and his FFI either.

Philippe persisted. In intense discussions over the better part of a week, he stressed to Guingouin that he was indifferent to local politics and cared only about winning the war. Even if the Salesman team represented the Allies, he argued, Guingouin ought to cooperate fully, just as the Russians were.

Jean Claude suggested trying flattery. The team radioed Baker Street and arranged for thousands of leaflets to be printed and airdropped throughout the region calling for "Allied active participation under Guingouin's leadership."

Guingouin was unmoved.

While negotiating with Guingouin, the Salesman agents did what they could with the men they had. Success bred success. As they showed that they could procure weapons in quantity, and that they could wield them with real expertise, more fighters joined up—especially after word spread about what *Das Reich* had done at Tulle and Oradour. Bob began sending out groups of trained guerrillas to blow up bridges and power lines on their own. The demand for armaments grew, which meant more and larger supply drops.

The Salesman agents set up encampments in the woods. They divided their *maquisard* volunteers into companies of sixty men. They allotted one Bren gun for every four fighters, and one antitank weapon—either an American bazooka or a British PIAT gun—for every ten. They appointed quartermasters and medics, and set up telephone lines linking the encampments to each other and to Philippe's headquarters in Sussac.

Jean Claude began scouting drop zones far afield from his rock hut. One day he took a bicycle and rode out to a likely spot he had heard about. He left his bike at the side of the road and made his way through a brushy thicket. Just as he was beginning to inspect the field that lay beyond it, he heard the sound of a truck. He turned and saw that it was a German patrol, drawing up alongside his bike. With no time to hide, he walked back to the roadside, ostentatiously buttoning his fly. He reflected that he was lucky the patrol was not French *Milice,* as they would have been suspicious of any Frenchman who moved into bushes to relieve himself when he could just as easily have done so by the side of the road.

It turned out that the soldiers weren't Germans either, but Wehrmacht conscripts from some conquered land, Jean Claude couldn't tell which. They demanded to see his papers. He handed over his forged identity card—the first time he had shown it to anyone. It passed muster.

The officer in charge asked Jean Claude in broken French what he was doing in the middle of nowhere with a Michelin map in his hand. Jean Claude, thanking his lucky stars that he hadn't marked the map, said he was searching for a farm he had heard about where he might find eggs, meat, and butter. The soldiers were excited to hear this, which created a complication: Jean Claude had to persuade them that he really didn't know where the farm was, and wasn't keeping its location from them. As he spun out his story, Jean Claude recalled later, he made an important discovery: His nervousness fell away, and he found himself lying with ease and conviction. He even showed his map to the commanding officer, asked where they were, and where he thought the farm might be. He was calm. Dissembling felt normal.

The soldiers got back into the truck, wished Jean Claude luck, and jokingly asked him to bring something back for them if he found the farm. Then they drove on.

In addition to his DZ duties, Jean Claude began to take part in roadside ambushes, though he was assigned to relatively safe positions. To his surprise, not all the targets were truck convoys; he was astonished at how much the German army still relied on horse-drawn vehicles. The main ambush weapons were the Sten gun and the Gammon bomb, a hand grenade with a canvas bag attached to it that could be filled with shrapnel, plastic explosive, or anything at hand. Gammons were effective at stopping vehicles and stunning soldiers, although Jean Claude found that German troops recovered quickly and responded with discipline. The ambushes seldom halted traffic for long, though they were able to slow it by forcing the Germans to use the confusing secondary roads.

Jean Claude also helped Bob, on occasion, teach recruits how to handle their new weapons. Guns arrived packed in Cosmoline, a sticky grease, which had to be laboriously removed with soap and water because gasoline, the preferred solvent, was scarce. Jean Claude didn't know the French words for many of the weapons' parts, but he could demonstrate how to strip, clean, and reassemble them. He also showed trainees how to handle TNT, plastics, Primacord, blasting caps, fuses, fog signals, and other instruments of demolition.

By late June Bob's squads of saboteurs had blown bridges at

Saint-Germain and Pierre-Buffière. They destroyed high-tension power lines, cutting off the electricity supply for the submarine base at Rochefort. And they blew up so many railroad tracks on their nightly raids that northbound rail traffic—from Bordeaux and Toulouse to Limoges and Paris—was significantly impaired.

The trouble with severing railroad tracks was that they wouldn't stay severed. It typically took the Germans no more than two days to repair them. For this they used a truly monstrous machine: an armored train, fitted with machine guns, that pushed ahead of it a flatcar carrying hostages. It would rumble up to the site of a breach and off-load new sections of track, which workers would fix in place. The train was impervious to small-arms fire. Bob and Philippe nicknamed it "*La Casserole.*"

A tip from an informer gave Philippe the idea for a way to do lasting damage to the major railway line connecting Paris and Toulouse. The line had two parallel sets of tracks. The informer, a railroad employee, reported that two Nazi trains were scheduled to pass each other in a deep cut—a man-made gorge—south of Salon-la-Tour, the village where Violette was captured. It was a tricky spot: The two sets of tracks made a tight turn through the cut, which had high, nearly vertical sides. The northbound train would be making a steep climb, the southbound one a slow descent.

Philippe and Bob rounded up thirty men and moved out to Salon-la-Tour, about twenty miles from Sussac. They skirted the village and continued on another half mile or so to the gorge. They posted lookouts in a wide circle. Philippe, Bob, and three others entered the cut and walked to its midpoint. They buried an enormous quantity of plastic explosive beneath the tracks. They ran detonator wires under gravel and weeds to plungers they concealed in bushes. Philippe ordered the men to scatter once the charge had blown, and meet at a rendezvous point he selected.

Less than an hour later two trains appeared, one at each end of the gorge. They were big ones, moving slowly through the narrow space. Once they overlapped, the saboteurs pushed the plungers. For a long moment they couldn't see what happened—the blast was so powerful that it created a vast cloud of thick dust, filling the gorge completely. When the dust began to settle, a twisted mass of steaming iron and steel slowly came into view. Both engines lay on their sides, crippled—and right across the two sets of tracks. The attackers fled in triumph.

It was eight long weeks before the Germans could reach the cut with rail cranes big enough to move the demolished locomotives and finally clear the tracks. During that time the northbound movement of Nazi tanks and troops was diverted to auxiliary tracks and roads, which the Salesman *maquisards* ambushed daily.

The show of force at Salon-la-Tour was followed in short order by another, even more important breakthrough. Whether motivated by the impressive scale of that attack, or by a shortage of supplies, or by a sense that much was beginning to be accomplished without him—or by a combination of all three—Georges Guingouin decided to cast his lot with Operation Salesman. Guingouin "was very bold and outspoken in his desire to collaborate with me on the condition that I had no political motive," Philippe wrote afterward in a report to Baker Street. "I was just as bold, and stated that I was only interested in winning the war, and that providing that he undertook to attend to all targets which I might designate, I would arm his troops to the best of our ability. After some arguing he accepted the agreement, and from that day he has never failed to execute immediately all orders from London, as well as to attend to all targets."

23

Operation Salesman II was still engaging in what would today be called asymmetric warfare—chiefly ambushes, sabotage, and sniping—but the team now commanded enough men at arms to make things hot for *Das Reich* troops whenever they ventured out from the safety of Limoges. Attacks were intentionally random. Often a single guerrilla, or a small band, would spot German uniforms in a town square or a country lane, cut a volley loose, and then immediately blend into the background. Larger groups of *maquisards* began to engage enemy patrols in firefights, which grew in duration and intensity. The Germans began to refer to the Limousin as "Little Russia." For safety they took to moving in armored convoys.

Jean Claude was especially impressed by the method devised for assaulting these convoys by a pair of cold-eyed Spaniards, part of a contingent of fierce Spanish Republican refugees. Known as Estavard and Franco, they had fought long and hard against the fascists in Spain's vicious civil war. They had lost everyone and everything they loved in that conflict and had fled to France, joining the *maquis* two years before the Salesman agents parachuted in. Much of their combat experience in Spain had been at close quarters, with knives. They wore faded, filthy berets, and they had scars on the weathered skin of their faces and arms. It seemed to Jean Claude that there was not much humanity left within them, only a silent, savage determination to kill Nazis.

Estavard and Franco had an old Citroën. They cut away the car's roof, leaving a narrow metal remnant over the doors and windshield frame. The glass was long gone. The two men would build up explosive devices out of Gammon bombs, strapping several together and loading them with jagged bits of iron. They placed these in baskets, one on the Citroën's front seat, one in back. Then they invited a couple of other *maquisards* to join them, loaded up the car with Sten guns and extra clips, and drove off in search of a German convoy.

They preferred to start their assault at the top of a hill. When they spotted a convoy coming up toward them, Estavard and the others stood on the backseat, Sten guns held low. Franco, at the wheel, took off down the hill, ramming the car through the gears. The moment they reached the lead vehicle, they opened fire at point-blank range. Then they sped along the convoy, firing Stens and hurling their enhanced grenades. Vehicles burst into flames and exploded. Nazi soldiers jumped out of trucks and half-tracks, some wounded, some on fire, a few shooting back.

The run at the convoy would be over quickly. If they had done enough damage they would turn around and slowly drive back alongside the destroyed vehicles, firing at any remaining targets. Occasionally Estavard went in with his knife to finish up.

Jean Claude always wondered why an enemy vehicle didn't simply pull out into the Citroen's lane, which would have stopped the assault in its tracks. But it never happened. Estavard and Franco both survived the war, though Jean Claude couldn't imagine what became of them afterward.

Strokes like these emboldened the Resistance. So too did reports from Normandy that the invasion was holding. In the Limousin, as everywhere in France, people were ready to avenge their occupation.

After Guingouin and his men joined the Salesman agents, their secret army grew quickly to about ten thousand fighters. They estimated that another five or six thousand volunteers were waiting to join them, if only they could obtain enough weapons. Deliveries by late June were averaging two planeloads a night. Jean Claude sent frequent messages to Baker Street asking for more.

One night toward the end of June, London sent a message via the late Morse Broadcast alerting the Salesman team to get ready to receive a large delivery. The message stressed that it was to be a daylight drop. This had never happened before. The novelty, and the prospect of receiving enough arms to relieve their shortage, prompted general exuberance. For a drop zone the agents chose a big open field on top of a high plateau, right in the center of their territory, near a little village called Domps. London confirmed that the drop would be made on June 25, sometime after 10:00 A.M.

On the evening of June 24, Jean Claude, Philippe, and a handful of *maquisards* sat quietly around the wireless set in the old mill, listening to the Broadcast for final instructions. There was static that night, making it difficult to hear clearly. The BBC announcer concluded the French newscast. The opening notes of Beethoven's Fifth Symphony were played, and then a voice began to enunciate the coded, seemingly random, *messages personnels*.

The men around the wireless became alert when the announcer said the code word for the Domps drop zone. Then, through the crackle, they heard: "We repeat, seventy-two times. . . ."

The men stared at one another. Could it possibly be? Seventy-two planeloads of weapons? They were by no means certain that they had heard correctly. Some thought they had heard "*soixante-douze*" (seventy-two), but others were certain that they had heard "*douze*" (twelve). Still others were convinced that they had heard "*soixante*" (sixty). They talked it over excitedly and concluded that the higher numbers couldn't possibly be correct. But they had no time to radio London for confirmation, so they set about rounding up what was for them a huge reception committee—enough men and vehicles to carry away a large number of planeloads, possibly greater than twelve, though almost certainly short of seventy-two.

Word spread quickly. By 8:00 the next morning, in addition to the reception committee, hundreds of civilians—men, women, and children—filtered out of the forest onto the plateau to see the show. Within an hour, three very large signal fires burned in a straight line down the plateau's center. Piles of grass, hay, and green cuttings were stacked next to the blazes, ready to be tossed onto the flames to indicate the wind direction. The civilians made an ebullient, noisy ring around the edge of the DZ.

Jean Claude was so accustomed to nighttime drops that without thinking about it he stood by the fire at the head of the line with a flashlight in his hand, ready to give the Morse recognition signal. He was expecting the usual Liberators or Lancasters to come in low, one at a time.

Instead, shortly after 10:00, there came a distant roar. Reception committee men threw greenery onto the fires, converting them to smoke pots. Jean Claude looked up and saw planes flying so high they looked like toys, higher than he had ever seen planes before, at perhaps five thousand feet. There were seventy-two of them—American B-17 Flying Fortress bombers—flying in tight formation.

The crowd on the ground erupted in cheers as clouds of parachutes opened and drifted down. Onlookers surged onto the drop zone, then quickly retreated when they saw that some containers were dropping like bombs, bouncing and breaking open as they hit the ground. The B-17 aircrews, with their sophisticated Norden bombsights, aimed their canisters far more accurately than the Americans who had made nighttime drops, but they still sometimes forgot to attach the static lines. Five or six dozen containers fell untethered. One landed near the spot where Jean Claude stood, bounced, broke open, and spilled

Operation Zebra, the first daytime drop of armaments to Resistance fighters
in France, took place on June 25, 1944. Half of the delivery went to
the Salesman circuit on a plateau near Domps, pictured here.

its load of ammunition into a fire. Very soon, as people stared up in wonder at the hundreds of parachutes floating peacefully down, exploding ammunition amplified the general excitement.

Just as the last of the bombers passed overhead, two P-51 Mustang fighters flew down to buzz the steep edge of the plateau. As they flashed past, flying so low that the spectators were almost at eye level with the pilots, a group of *maquis* fighters stood at present arms. The pilots waggled their wings in response.

Then the reception committee got to work. The trucks the guerrillas had brought to cart away the containers were far too few for the job, so civilians fetched farm wagons drawn by horses and oxen and merrily helped out. (The parachutes themselves, made of precious silk, were rolled up and taken away for wives and girlfriends.) It took days to locate all the containers and move them to central collection points. When they were counted, the Salesman agents found that they had received a staggering 860 containers.

Jean Claude and the others didn't know it, but they had just taken part in a milestone in the war—Operation Zebra, the Allies' first daytime supply drop in Europe. The delivery was made by a massive armada of 180 B-17 bombers from the 3rd Air Division, flying out of Suffolk, escorted by Mustangs and P-47 Thunderbolts. In Operation Zebra, weapons and supplies were dropped to Resistance groups in four locations in France. Nearly half went to the Salesman circuit.

As the reception committee collected the supplies and carried them away, a squad of men was assigned to gather the containers that had been damaged when their parachutes failed to open. Among these they found two that, in a freak accident, had smashed together and broken open at the edge of the DZ. One was fully loaded with C-4 plastic explosive. In the other were small wooden boxes containing carefully packaged blasting caps. The boxes had shattered, and in the commingled mess, loose caps had become embedded in the exposed explosive. If the caps were stepped on, or even gripped too tightly, the whole works could explode. But the reception party knew how desperately the *maquisards* needed those blasting caps. Without requesting authorization, because he was certain Philippe would refuse it, Jean Claude helped two other Resistance men gingerly pick the caps out of the C-4.

24

With Guingouin's men and London's arms, the Salesman agents were now in command of a large guerrilla army. They grouped the fighters in three main encampments—"hedgehogs," Jean Claude called them, military shorthand for mutually supporting strongpoints—in a ring around Limoges: one to the southeast, one to the southwest, and one to the northwest. They worked out a system for purchasing, storing, and distributing food. The whole operation was overseen by Philippe, and sustained by supply drops that Jean Claude coordinated with London over his wireless set. He was still anxious every time he switched it on. A small plane had started making frequent flights overhead within a week of his arrival; once or twice it even seemed to circle.

After the June 25 daylight drop, the pace of assaults and demolitions grew ferocious. By the first week in July, Operation Salesman had won effective control of a big swath of terrain: all of the Haute-Vienne department outside Limoges; most of the Corrèze; and parts of the Creuse, Dordogne, and Charente departments. Many times each day, the countryside rang with the sounds of collapsing bridges, detonated railroad tracks, and attacks on northbound German troops. It didn't take long for the *maquisards* to run through the explosives and ammunition they had received. Moonlit nights were busy; drops came at a rate of between four and eight per night in July. Operation Salesman received some 1,600 containers that month, and still it wasn't enough.

Now more than ever, Jean Claude wanted to get out of his rock hut and into battle. Philippe and Bob had worn their uniforms since arriving in France, for the faint possibility of protection they might provide in case of capture, and also presumably for the aura of command they conveyed. Jean Claude, who was supposed to remain inconspicuous, had worn his civilian clothing. But now he availed himself of an enlisted man's olive-drab uniform that arrived in one of the drops. Somewhere he found insignia, a second lieutenant's bar and a U.S. insignia, but only one of each, rather than the two required. It wasn't until the following month that he was able to get properly outfitted—and to obtain, at last, a pair of the jump boots he longed for.

After much hounding, Philippe finally consented in early July to give Jean Claude a combat role—on the condition that he train a qualified, London-approved wireless operator to take his place. That sounded like a tall order, considering all the preparation Jean Claude had undergone to qualify for Operation Salesman. But he set about training a pair of assistants who knew some Morse code. Jean Claude handled the enciphering and deciphering of messages, while the assistants began receiving the Broadcast.

Then Jean Claude had a fantastic stroke of luck. He came across a man, identified only as André, who had served as the wireless operator for General Maxime Weygand, the commander of the French army at the time of the surrender in 1940. André was proficient in Morse. After conferring at length with Baker Street, Jean Claude gave him a crash course in SOE communications protocol. Baker Street tested André's competence and recorded his "fist." Before long André was decoding messages, and in time he was encoding as well. Jean Claude retained responsibility for inserting the security identifiers into

SOE agents in Sussac on the morning of July 9, 1944, including members
of a circuit code-named Tilleul, who parachuted in the night before.
Jean Claude is third from left; Bob is second from right; Jacques Dufour
is at far right; and at center, giving the V for victory sign, is Jacques de Guelis.

messages, but André took over a good portion of the transmissions. He spoke no English, but it made no difference, as long as he was able to convert one set of symbols to another accurately and swiftly. Jean Claude had "managed to transform myself into [Philippe's] personal reserve communication link," he wrote later.

André was kept busy transmitting requests for arms drops to London. The need for fresh weapons kept growing, especially as the emboldened *maquisards* began augmenting their hit-and-run guerrilla tactics with more conventional kinds of warfare, like sending out patrols to hunt for Germans. Baker Street sent instructions to destroy a towering railway viaduct at Pierre-Buffière, and to sabotage wolfram mines near Saint-Léonard and Bellac. (Wolframite was the main source of tungsten, useful for making armor-piercing ammunition.)

Just as the *maquisards* in central France were coalescing into a real fighting force early that July, however, the invading armies in Normandy reached a precarious point. Allied troops had clawed their way ashore and secured beachheads, but when they tried to push inland they ran into an unexpected obstacle. For centuries, Norman farmers had cultivated land using dense, tall hedges—*bocages*—with sunken lanes running behind them, to separate pastures. The hedgerows served many purposes—controlling water, blocking wind, penning cattle—but now they turned out to have another attribute: They gave the Germans an almost ideal defense against Allied tanks.

The Allies could neither see over the hedgerows nor maneuver through them. The Germans, on the other hand, were able to employ the country lanes as trenches. They fired at the lightly armored undersides of Sherman tanks using the *Panzerfaust,* a weapon that was like an American bazooka, only better. Eventually, U.S. combat engineers hit upon the idea of welding long, steel "tusks" to the fronts of tanks, and these "rhino tanks" were able to tear through the hedgerows. But that took time. More than a month after D-Day, the Allies were still bottled up in Normandy, trying to break through the German defenses at Saint-Lô and Caen. It became a matter of vital importance to deliver arms in quantity to the *maquisards* behind the lines, enabling them to delay German reinforcements and occupy the maximum number of enemy troops.

On the morning of July 14, Bastille Day, nine wings of American B-17s—more than 320 bombers in all—took off from nine air bases in East Anglia and gathered in a massive formation over southern England. Approaching the English Channel they were joined by a huge fighter escort—328 Mustangs and 196 Thunderbolts. It was an astonishing show of air superiority: crossing into France in the early morning light, the parade of planes looked to some on the ground like a gleaming constellation on the move. Passing southwest of Paris, the formation was attacked by a squadron of Messerschmitt Bf 109 fighters; the Americans swatted them out of the sky. When they reached the Loire Valley, the bombers split into groups and dropped 3,780 containers—nearly 500 tons of supplies—to seven *maquis* contingents.

Jean Claude, Philippe, and Bob received their share of the drop—thirty-five planeloads—at a DZ on a high plateau near Sussac, in the foothills of Mont Gargan. In many ways it was a replay of the first daylight drop. The reception committee lit bonfires on the plateau (Jean Claude did not bring a flashlight this time). Excited civilians ringed the DZ. When the men tending the fires heard the high-altitude throb of the B-17s, they threw greenery into the flames to make smoke signals. As before, some containers whose static lines had been left unhooked came crashing down and broke open, spilling loose ammunition into a bonfire.

In one important way, however, this drop was different. As hundreds of parachutes bloomed high overhead, the people on the ground gasped with surprise and delight. The parachutes were blue, white, and red—a tribute to the flag of France, and to the Resistance. They hung suspended for a long time, as they were deployed at such a high altitude. A couple of American fighter planes flew down low and

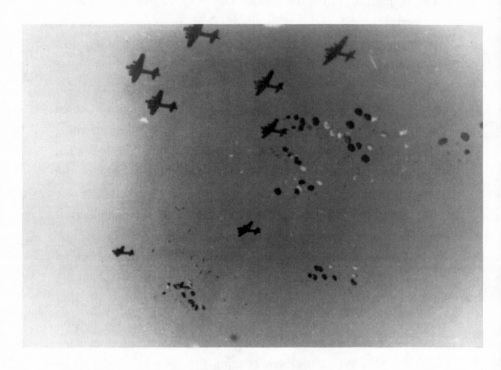

On July 14, 1944—Bastille Day—Allied bombers delivered the largest arms drop of the war, using blue, white, and red parachutes, the colors of the French flag. A provocation the Nazis couldn't abide, it sparked a ferocious enemy response.

buzzed the edge of the plateau. This time the Frenchmen on the ground sang "La Marseillaise."

The Bastille Day drop, the largest of the war, was code-named Operation Cadillac. In France it is remembered as the *parachutage tricolore*, after the name of the French flag. Like people all around the country who witnessed it, the Salesman agents were moved and impressed. Which of their London spymasters, they wondered, had dreamed up such a boost to morale?

They never found out. Before long, however, they were cursing him.

25

When the last of the parachutes had floated to the ground, and the canisters had been rounded up and collected in a central spot, the reception committee counted and found that there were 410 of them. Many were opened up so that their contents could be verified and decisions could be made about their distribution. One package was addressed to Jean Claude. It contained a complete spare radio set, a bag of rice, and—best of all—a large chunk of semisweet chocolate.

The removal of the canisters from the plateau went slowly. The novelty and urgency were not as great as they had been with the first daylight drop, and *maquisards* preferred ambushing German road traffic to serving as stevedores. By the end of the day most of the canisters were still there (though all the silk parachutes had disappeared). Jean Claude took his things and returned to Sussac to check on any messages André had decoded in his absence. He savored some of his chocolate, "a rather small piece of which," he wrote later, "I ungenerously managed to part with" and give to André.

The sorting and removal of the containers didn't go any more quickly over the next two days. A shortage of charcoal meant that few *gazogene* trucks were available. By the evening of the sixteenth, about half the drop remained on the DZ, waiting to be sorted and distributed.

The next morning, July 17, Jean Claude heard gunfire. It came from the direction of La Croisille, to the southwest, and it sounded different from skirmishes he had heard before—the firing was more intense, and lasted longer. André was absent, and Philippe did not make his usual morning appearance at the rock hut. Worried, Jean Claude carried his new wireless set to a stand of bushes and trees a few hundred feet behind the hut and hid it in a crevice under a rock outcrop. Then he packed his old set into its suitcase. He gathered up his crystals, code sheets, paper, magnifying glass, and pencils, and put them in a small leather satchel. He waited awhile, listening to the gunfire, which ebbed and flowed but never stopped. Still Philippe did not come. Jean Claude picked up the suitcase and the satchel and set out on foot for the DZ, a distance of about four miles over narrow forest paths.

He found Philippe at an edge of the clearing, looking concerned. Reports of enemy activity were coming in from all over the Salesman II territory, none of them good. The attack at La Croisille had been the first German thrust. A little later, two thousand German troops had begun moving toward them from the southeast, near the Plateau de Millevaches. By the afternoon the agents learned of more attacks from the west, around Linards, and from the east, at Beaumont. The Germans, it appeared, were beginning a full-scale *ratissage*—a sweep of the area, aiming to wipe out the guerrillas once and for all and clear the way for *Das Reich*'s northward march.

Jean Claude and Philippe speculated that the provocation had been the *parachutage tricolore*. Such a blatant act of patriotic opposition, they figured, could not go unanswered by the occupiers. They shared some choice words for whatever fool had brought the wrath of the SS upon them.

Jean Claude assembled his old wireless set and threw its antenna up over a tree branch. He sent messages to Baker Street indicating that a general assault was under way. At Philippe's direction, he also sent a request for shock troops. Then, as evening approached, he packed the wireless set back in its suitcase, left it at the DZ, and walked back to Sussac. That night he retrieved his second radio from its hiding place and set it up in the rock hut. He sent messages to London canceling drops to several DZs that were now unusable, as the enemy was too close.

In the morning, Jean Claude returned to the plateau to help with the remaining containers. He was needed, as many of the men assigned to the reception committee had reported back to their units to defend against German advances. Those who remained loaded containers onto the few trucks and carts available. Late in the afternoon, some trucks that had left the plateau to deliver canisters to a *maquis* group near Saint-Yrieix-la-Perche, thirty miles to the southwest, returned—still fully loaded. Their crews reported that the route was blocked by German soldiers. Jean Claude walked back to the rock hut and turned in for the night.

It was early the next morning when the *feldgrau* truck roared up to his door.

26

Jean Claude had the presence of mind to grab his crystals, codes, and schedules before leaping through the hut's rear window and hiding in the underbrush. There was no time to do anything about the wireless set. German soldiers jumped down from the truck yelling *"Raus! Raus!"* and stormed in through the front door.

Jean Claude was close enough to hear the soldiers' happy exclamations when they found his rice and *"schokolade."* He lay still while they ransacked the hut. It didn't take them long, as the place was so small. Jean Claude saw them hustle back to the truck with his wireless set and all the loose papers they had found.

When the truck had driven away, Jean Claude got to his feet and went deeper into the woods. He thought he should head for the DZ, to find Philippe and report to Baker Street, but in his shaken state he wanted to avoid roads and trails. He made his way slowly through the trees, circling the Sussac village, in the direction of the plateau.

In the forest, he came across a group of about twenty Salesman *maquisards*. They were on their way to help another group that had ambushed a German armored car and wanted to use the wreck to set up a roadblock.

Jean Claude joined them, and before long they came to the site of the ambush. The armored car, destroyed by bazooka fire and Gammon grenades, lay tipped on its side across the road. A couple of corpses lay amid the mangled mess inside. As the guerrillas rummaged around for souvenirs and talked over the assault, Jean Claude learned that two German soldiers had survived and were being held prisoner in a clearing at a little distance. He thought he might interrogate them about the enemy's movements, using the very little German he had studied as a college freshman.

After a short hike down a forest trail, accompanied by a few Sussac *maquisards,* Jean Claude found the prisoners in the custody of some of the Spanish Republicans. The captives were seated on the ground, hands and feet bound, with Primacord explosive wrapped around their necks. The Spaniards sat about a hundred yards away, drinking wine. Between the Germans and their captors crackled a long, slow fuse, spitting sparks.

Jean Claude protested. He suggested offering the men a chance to live, in exchange for information. The Spaniards resisted. The confrontation became heated, but in the end Jean Claude, backed by his Sussac men, prevailed.

He cut the fuse and removed the Primacord from the prisoners' necks. In rudimentary German, he told them that he was an American soldier, and that they would be protected if they answered his questions. They were clearly shocked—they couldn't imagine encountering an American so deep in occupied France. But as it turned out, they had little information of any use to share.

No sooner was the standoff settled than they heard the sound of an engine. It was a *feldgrau* truck, heading up the road behind them toward the spot where the shattered armored car lay. Jean Claude and the *maquisards* raced back to join the ambush that was being hurriedly assembled. A guerrilla who had picked up a German Schmeisser machine pistol handed Jean Claude his carbine.

The truck came around a curve and its driver spotted the ruined armored car. He skidded to a stop immediately, much farther away than the guerrillas had anticipated. As troops jumped out, the *maquisards* opened fire. The truck backed up out of sight around the curve. The German troops gave very heavy return fire, retreated to the truck, and jumped aboard. Under a final burst from the guerrillas, the truck turned around and drove off.

The engagement lasted only a brief moment. When it was done, the *maquisards* went to work setting up a strong roadblock with the armored car as its centerpiece. It occurred to Jean Claude that this was a new kind of combat for them—defending a set position—a departure from their usual fluid, guerrilla tactics. It was a type of warfare for which neither he nor the *maquisards* had trained, but it would be necessary if they were to keep the enemy from overrunning the DZ on the plateau.

Jean Claude handed the carbine back and set off for the DZ on foot.

27

Jean Claude found a *maquis* commander directing a group working furiously to load canisters onto trucks and carts. The sound of small arms fire came from all directions, continual and close by. The commander swore when Jean Claude told him about the armored car, the German truck, and the ambushes. He directed his crew to carry some containers off into the woods around the plateau, six men to a canister, and hide them in ditches and hollows, camouflaging them with brush. Jean Claude pitched in and worked all day.

Late in the afternoon a runner dashed onto the DZ, out of breath. He reported that his unit was heavily engaged by a German force on a major roadway leading up to the DZ, very near Sussac. They urgently needed ammunition, grenades, and reinforcements, he said. A dozen men grabbed weapons and scrambled aboard one of the trucks that hadn't been able to reach its destination—it was already loaded with boxes of ammunition, bandoliers, and grenades. Jean Claude thought for a moment. He had had enough of moving containers. The truck, he told himself, would be heading near where Philippe was thought to be. He took a Bren gun and a couple of extra clips out of a container. Jean Claude climbed onto the truck with the others.

The drive over winding back roads was bumpy, tense, and short.

The sound of gunfire grew louder as the truck progressed. The truck stopped on the side of a gentle foothill, part of a formation rising to high mountains in the distance. Gunfire seemed to be coming from the other side of the hill.

The runner wanted to lead the men around the hill to his unit. Jean Claude suggested that it would be a better idea to climb to the top and have a look over. The others agreed, and they hustled up to a spot on the ridgeline between two sharp rock projections a good four hundred yards apart. Below them lay a steep, sparsely forested incline. A road ran along its base. It was there that a large contingent of German troops and a group of *maquisards* had blundered into one another. They were engaged in a ferocious, confused firefight.

Sten guns would be useless at this range, but not Jean Claude's Bren. The light machine gun, a squad assault weapon, was a mainstay of Britain's infantry—it fired standard .303-caliber rifle rounds and had an effective range of six hundred yards. With its curved, top-mounted, 30-round magazine, it had a slower rate of fire than a belt-fed machine gun, but it was easier to move around. Jean Claude carried his weapon about halfway down the hill, accompanied by the other men from the DZ.

They found cover behind rocks and trees and opened fire into the German flank. The *maquisards* on the road understood what was happening and extended their position up the hill until the two forces joined. Together they unleashed a tremendous fusillade down into the enemy position. Visibility through the trees was poor, but they could see that the terrain on the far side of the road was difficult, with a small swamp, dense brush, and a steep slope. The enemy had nowhere to go.

The Germans returned fire with rifles and automatic weapons, but before long they began to retreat. They didn't break off exactly, they moved back methodically, maintaining aggressive contact, probing for fresh approaches. Then, just before sundown, the shooting ceased.

Jean Claude's blood fizzed with adrenaline. Looking back on the skirmish—his first real taste of combat—many years later, he didn't recall feeling much terror. That, he thought, was partly because the fighting had been at a distance, but also because some of his SOE training exercises had been scarier, even though nobody was trying to kill him. Mostly he felt satisfied that he had taken part and accomplished something.

He walked down to the road and found the commander of the *maquis* group there, who thanked him for the help. They discussed how best to fortify the roadblock. Jean Claude and the others in his group helped cut down trees and drag them into position across the road, left their unused ammunition with the defenders, and drove back to the DZ.

That night the men loaded the trucks and farm carts with fresh urgency. Philippe arrived around midnight. Jean Claude retrieved his wireless set from its hiding place—he was getting good at tossing his antenna into a tree and making transmissions crouched on the ground. Philippe gave him a message for Baker Street. Its gist was that a possible catastrophe was unfolding at Châteauneuf-la-Forêt, ten miles to the north. German troops had assaulted the town, and the *maquisards* there were determined to hold it. Philippe had insisted that they revert to fluid tactics, but the fighters, mindful of what had happened at Tulle and Oradour, had refused. Bob was in the thick of it. Philippe expected the defense "to go bust."

Philippe told Jean Claude to stay in the general area of the DZ and make sure the containers were distributed or saved. Then he vanished into the night.

28

By morning about thirty containers remained on the DZ. Jean Claude, who had napped from time to time during the night, could tell it was going to be a scorching day as soon as the sun came up. With the dawn came renewed gunfire, concentrated now in the north, southeast, and southwest.

Reports arrived of German assaults on several approaches to the DZ. The heaviest was at Châteauneuf. Another was at the site of the roadblock where Jean Claude had fought the day before. Again came requests for ammunition and reinforcements. Men rushed off to deliver armaments and join the defenders.

Jean Claude joined a group of about two dozen men heading back to the roadblock. They found a little truck and crammed it full of firearms, ammunition, and crate after crate of grenades.

Arriving at the back of the hill as they had the day before, they heard gunfire once again on the other side, though it had a different sound. The Germans had returned in force, and this time they had brought heavy machine guns. Jean Claude thought one of the rocky promontories he had noted the previous day might provide good cover, and he suggested that the men head there. The climb was made arduous by the crates of arms they carried, and by the growing heat.

The sight that greeted them from their vantage on the ridgeline was close to desperate—the *maquisards* down at the road were outnumbered and outgunned. The roadblock itself had changed hands; the Germans had overrun it and were now using it for cover. German soldiers, attempting to outflank the *maquis* position, were climbing up the slope below.

It was instantly clear to Jean Claude that they had to hold the high ground. He shouted to the men with Bren guns to take up positions around the rocky abutment. They complied.

At that moment, Jean Claude recalled afterward, he was struck by a thought that gave him a distinct twinge of fright: The other men were regarding him as their commander. He was, after all, the uniformed American who had parachuted in to help. They probably supposed he had more combat experience than they did, though the truth was almost certainly the reverse.

There was no time for hesitation. Trying to project a confidence he didn't feel, Jean Claude positioned men a little way down the slope, on the *maquis* side of the roadblock, to give some depth to the guerrillas' defenses and provide covering fire if they needed to retreat. He told them not to bunch up. He assigned two men to be runners, and two more to distribute ammunition and grenades. He sent several men to the rear, to guard against flanking actions from that direction.

From the promontory Jean Claude watched his second line form up behind rocks and trees and begin to add their supporting fire to the general din. He could see that the German soldiers climbing the hillside were stretched out and exposed. He gathered a small group and led them partway down, toward the rear of the German flank. At close range, they opened fire with automatic weapons and hurled grenades. The enemy troops began to fall back. In occasional lulls in the gunfire, Jean Claude heard them shouting. He realized that not all the men in German uniforms were German; they spoke in several languages, one of which he didn't recognize. The *maquisards* from the DZ forced most of the soldiers back down to the road, where they took cover behind the roadblock. Jean Claude immediately led his men back to the ridgeline.

Summoning his runners, he told them to spread the word: Concentrate fire on the German speakers, as they were undoubtedly the officers and noncoms.

Possibly because he was contemplating language, Jean Claude then had a thought that momentarily sickened him: He still had his codes and crystals in his pockets, as well as the schedules indicating the dates, times, and frequencies for his communications with Baker Street. He had a brief, nightmarish vision of what could happen if he was killed and the enemy searched his pockets. Others would be likely to die because of his indiscretion.

He didn't have time to dwell on it. The men were all suffering from thirst. The day was growing hotter by the hour, and the guerrillas, unaccustomed to pitched battles, had not thought to bring water. Jean Claude instructed a runner to drive the truck back to the DZ and return with water, more ammunition, and a status report on the clearance of the containers.

There came a lull in the fighting as the Germans regrouped in response to the initial, sharp attack on their flank. Jean Claude took advantage of it to pick his way down to the road and confer with the *maquisards* there. He set out with three men, scampering down the hill, hiding behind rocks and trees, slipping past isolated enemy positions and patrols. They were near the bottom when Jean Claude heard what sounded like a pistol shot. One of his men, wounded in the torso, collapsed. Jean Claude hit the ground and crawled forward. Seconds later he came across the body of a German soldier with what looked like knife wounds. One of his other men, he presumed, had found the shooter and stabbed him to death.

Jean Claude crept onward. He reached the roadside and found the guerrillas gathered there. He discovered that there were some five hundred of them, and was pleased to learn that very few had been wounded. Talking with their leaders, he suggested that they concentrate on holding the road and covering its far side; he would move some of his men partway down the hill and try to prevent the enemy from advancing by that route. He told them he would send down ammunition once the truck returned from the DZ.

Then he and his two companions set out back up the hill. Jean Claude never found out what happened to the wounded man.

It was late morning, and scorching hot, by the time they reached the ridgeline. Jean Claude repositioned his men in two defensive lines, one atop the hill and the other a little way down. There they waited, with Bren guns and crates of grenades.

The Germans repositioned their forces too during this period of relative calm. They brought in truckloads of fresh troops, and shifted heavy machine guns to emplacements with good cover and clear sight lines to the ridge.

When the German assault came, it was furious. It began with a sustained barrage from the machine guns aimed at the ridge. Then German soldiers began climbing. It was difficult going, as the slope was steep and gravelly, but there were a lot of them. Automatic fire raked the ground in front of the advancing men.

The *maquisards* returned fire with Bren guns and, when the soldiers got close enough, with Stens. Many of the enemy soldiers were wounded or killed, and bodies began to accumulate on the slope. But the sheer cyclic rate of fire of the German machine guns was overwhelming, and the *maquisard* gunners were frequently silenced for short periods, unable to do anything but take cover, while the German troops muscled up the hillside. The guerrillas positioned partway down the hill were forced to retreat to the second line up on the ridge.

But there they held. They had good cover—and the huge quantity of grenades they had brought from the DZ. These were effective only as far as they could be thrown, of course, but the *maquisards,* hurling them with abandon, were able to create a lethal hail of metal that the soldiers could not cross. The Germans halted their advance, and for a time the guns fell silent.

Jean Claude used the lull to distribute ammunition and grenades. Water was as much in demand as ammunition, but still there was none. Jean Claude and the others could see German troops moving about down by the roadblock, but couldn't make out what they were doing.

Then the German assault resumed. It began with the din of machine guns, once again raking the ground in front of advancing infantrymen. Then came an even more hellish sound. The Germans had brought up mortars.

Jean Claude and his men retreated a short way to take cover in a stand of trees behind the ridgeline. The Germans saw them move, and timed mortar rounds to explode in the treetops, producing an infernal storm of metal and splintered wood. Jean Claude moved from tree to tree, trying to find clear lines of sight to return fire, but as the barrage went on he sometimes found himself crouching, pressed tightly against a tree trunk, practically hugging it, in the hope that the big lower branches might protect him from the howling blizzard of shrapnel and splinters. Men around him screamed and died. Jean Claude was thoroughly terrified.

Machine-gun fire continued marching up the hill toward the ridgeline, and German soldiers followed it. Jean Claude could see that the position was about to be overrun. He led his men at a sprint back to the rocky outcrop, where they had left their precious cache of grenades. They popped up to throw grenades and fire at the advancing soldiers as best they could, changing positions frequently. The lead German soldiers were nearly at the ridge.

The enemy fire grew so intense that Jean Claude and his men could no longer leave cover to shoot back. They began blindly rolling grenades, as fast as they could, over the edge. They took whole crates of grenades, pulled a few of the pins, and slid the crates down the gravelly slope, greatly expanding the grenades' kill zone.

It was a desperate tactic, but it worked. The Germans broke off the assault. Firing became sporadic, and the surviving troops began sliding and running down the hill. *Maquisards* shot at the retreating soldiers, who took cover on the way down behind the corpses of their fallen comrades.

By the middle of the afternoon, only an occasional gunshot sounded. Some of the German soldiers held a position less than a quarter of the way up the hill. Most were back down by the road, sheltered by the roadblock or by two smoldering *feldgrau* trucks that evidently had been destroyed by the guerrillas there.

As sundown approached, Jean Claude expected the Germans to depart as they had done the day before. Instead, the mortar and heavy machine-gun fire started up again. A few German soldiers started back up the hill, but not nearly as many as before. Jean Claude had a bad suspicion.

His fear was confirmed when he heard firing behind him. German soldiers had crept around into the woods on the back side of the hill and were coming up from that direction. If not for the sentries posted there, the surprise would have been complete.

Jean Claude called for reinforcements and dashed toward the sound of firing. German soldiers had made it well up the slope, almost unopposed. Jean Claude and his men joined the sentries, took cover, and opened fire. They were badly overextended, but they managed to drive the soldiers off. As the sun went down, the shooting stopped.

Then Jean Claude heard a most welcome sound. It was the little truck, returning from the DZ. The runner had loaded it up with ammunition, more grenades, even some reinforcements—and, best of all, food and drink.

The runner also brought good news: He reported that the DZ was almost completely cleared. By midday tomorrow, he said, it would be an empty field, and there would no longer be any need to hold the road. Jean Claude began to consider a new course of action while he oversaw the distribution of the food and drink and placed the new men in the area of the last attack. He told the runner to take some wounded men back to the DZ in the truck, and then return with more supplies, and more reinforcements if possible.

The news from the DZ, and the provisions, were a huge boost to morale. The men had had nothing to eat or drink all day. The truck had brought some water, but far more wine and cider, in small casks and bottles. Jean Claude was a bit concerned at the thought of thirsty men drinking wine like water, but he noticed no ill effects.

He needn't have worried. The *maquisards*, living in the woods for so long, had periodically suffered outbreaks of waterborne diseases. For many of them, the only safe liquid for years had been wine.

When it was dark, Jean Claude slipped down the hill again to confer with the *maquisard* leaders by the road. They all agreed that with the DZ nearly cleared, they should disengage the next day. But they had to figure out how—this kind of fighting was new to most of them. They worked out a plan to spread out and fall back in stages, with groups of men retreating under covering fire, then turning around to provide cover for those they had passed. They made decisions about positions, routes, and timing. As Jean Claude, up on the ridgeline, would have the best overall view, he was to give the signal: the detonation of several blocks of plastic explosive, which made a distinctive boom.

Once the arrangements were agreed upon, Jean Claude climbed back to his position. He drank some wine. In the quiet dark, he was overcome by exhaustion, but he also felt a certain ease. He had been frightened all day, especially during the mortar attack. But he had survived, and he had not panicked. Perhaps influenced by the wine, he felt something like happiness. He slept.

29

J ean Claude awoke in the faint early dawn to the sound of resuming German gunfire. He heard trucks approaching too, most likely bringing enemy reinforcements.

Skirmishing lasted for most of the morning. The Germans raked the ridge with automatic fire, and again they deployed mortars. Jean Claude's men ran low on ammunition. German troops launched a hard assault against the *maquis* position by the roadblock. By noon it looked as if the guerrillas might not hold.

Jean Claude saw no sense in trying—surely the DZ would be cleared by now. He detonated the blocks of plastic explosive. As the blast resounded over the battleground, the *maquisards* began to fade away.

The German machine-gun and mortar fire abruptly ceased. The *maquisards* fell back in groups, running through the trees, then pausing to provide covering fire for those who followed. Jean Claude was amazed at how smoothly the extrication progressed. The Germans made no attempt to follow the retreating men.

Suddenly Jean Claude understood why. Another *maquis* group, having no inkling of the withdrawal plan, had at that moment arrived at the other side of the German position and attacked from behind.

Surprised and grateful for the diversion, Jean Claude led his men away into the safety of the forest.

That night they had a tired celebration in the woods, with plenty to eat and drink. They talked over the German attack. None of them could understand its persistence. If the Germans had been so intent on reaching the DZ, why hadn't they disengaged and found another route? The only explanation they could think of was that the troops had been assigned to that sector and, once engaged, would not let go. Someone in charge, they figured, was not going to admit being unable to deal with a bunch of irregulars.

Later, Jean Claude learned that his firefight was one front in what has come to be called the battle of Mont Gargan, a broad defense by about 3,800 *maquisards* against an assault by 4,800 German troops—some of them SS, including Romanian and Russian conscripts—and about 500 French *Milice*. It lasted the better part of a week. Casualties were lopsided: 342 German soldiers were killed or wounded, while of the *maquisards*, 38 were killed, 54 were wounded, and 5 disappeared. The battle is remembered as a major success for the Resistance—not a victory exactly, as the guerrillas slipped away when the fighting was done—but an important holding action that protected the arms drop and helped divert *Das Reich* from its northward march. In France, it is commemorated as a milestone military achievement—for Georges Guingouin and his Communist Party fighters.

Jean Claude stayed with his little band of DZ *maquisards* for another day. Word reached them that Philippe had given instructions to revert to guerrilla tactics—to harry any German patrols and destroy what they could, but not to hold terrain. Jean Claude took part in a couple of ambushes, and late in the day he handed his Bren gun to one of the other fighters, left the group, and walked back to the DZ. He retrieved his wireless set from its hiding place and took it back to the rock hut at Sussac. There he contacted Philippe by telephone and recounted what he had seen and done during the days they had been out of touch.

Philippe expressed satisfaction that Jean Claude had survived and "enjoyed himself." Jean Claude learned that the Châteauneuf position had been overrun, but that Bob was unhurt. Philippe told Jean Claude to sit tight and expect him soon.

The next morning a two-car convoy pulled up in front of the rock hut. In the first car were Guingouin and two of his top aides. Philippe was at the wheel of the second car, and Bob sat beside him. Jean Claude loaded his wireless set into Philippe's car. They drove off with Guingouin in the lead.

For two hours they motored along roads that were little more than wide pathways through the woods. Philippe drove with brio—he had done some amateur road racing before the war. At one point they came to an intersection where their path through the trees crossed a larger dirt road. Jean Claude saw dust in the air. The cars zipped through, and Jean Claude saw that they were driving in the dust cloud raised by the wheels of *feldgrau* trucks that had crossed on the bigger road seconds before. If the Germans saw the cars they didn't give chase. Jean Claude doubted that their trucks could have fit on the narrow forest trail in any case.

They arrived at last at a clearing in the woods where an isolated farmhouse stood, one of Guingouin's hideouts. They were to spend a few days there, collecting intelligence and making fresh plans. Guingouin, his aides, and the Salesman agents gathered around a table and spread out a large map of the region. Each man marked it with what he knew about the Nazi offensive. As the big picture emerged, they were shocked by the scale of the assault. The Germans seemed to be letting up on the Haute-Vienne, but they were sending more troops into the surrounding departments—Charente, Creuse, and Corrèze.

Philippe told them that he had appealed to Baker Street to send an

OG—short for Operational Group. OGs were OSS commando teams, under joint command with SOE, specially trained in small-unit tactics for the post–D-Day phase of the war. Each OG consisted of two officers and fifteen enlisted men, selected for their language proficiency and toughness. They fought in uniform, and as a rule they were lethally effective—in an ambush in the Vercors that July, one team killed more than a hundred German soldiers in ten minutes. Philippe intended to use an OG as the spearhead of a counteroffensive against the German *ratissage*.

Until the OG arrived, Philippe thought it best to exploit the essential advantage that guerrilla armies have held since the dawn of warfare: the ability to vanish. He gave orders for the *maquisards* to melt into the countryside and let the Germans roam freely, believing they had accomplished their mission. Resupply drops were curtailed, and save for the occasional ambush at the territory's perimeter, enemy patrols went unmolested.

Jean Claude had little to do at the farmhouse. He monitored the Broadcast and kept up scheduled wireless contacts with London. He and Bob went for walks together, never venturing far from the farm.

One day the two men were walking along a narrow dirt road when they heard the sound of trucks. They ran a short distance off the road and dove into a stand of tall, thick grass that was partly covered by overhanging bushes. They had just a few seconds to burrow into the undergrowth before two trucks came abreast of them. The trucks stopped. Jean Claude and Bob were certain they were about to be killed or taken prisoner. But the enemy troops—French *Milice* and "German-Allied" conscripts, led by German noncoms—climbed down from the trucks, stretched, lit cigarettes, and relieved themselves by the roadside. They were just stopping for a ten-minute break.

Jean Claude and Bob lay perfectly still. They were so close that they were both sprayed by enemy urine. From what they saw and heard, it was clear that the soldiers were perfectly at ease, unafraid that they might be attacked. The troops remounted the trucks and drove on.

The episode was happenstance, but it could hardly have been a more perfect illustration, in miniature, of the tactical state of affairs. All around the Salesman territory, *maquisards* went to ground but did not depart. The German commanders, with no one to fight, became convinced that they had wiped out the guerrillas. Within a week they began withdrawing troops and moving them to the north and east—just as the Allied invaders were finally clearing the hedgerows in Normandy and preparing to deliver a hammer blow to the Nazi occupiers. The anvil was on the way: More Allied troops were heading for France's Mediterranean coast, preparing to come ashore at Cavalaire, Saint-Tropez, and Saint-Raphael, in a giant reinforcing movement that is sometimes called "the Forgotten Campaign."

30

Sometime during those closing weeks of July, or perhaps in early August, Violette Szabo scratched her name into the wall of cell number 45 at 84 avenue Foch.

Beyond that, few details are known for certain about Violette's imprisonment and interrogation in Paris. Some chroniclers have claimed she was atrociously tortured but managed to stay silent, even defiant. Others have found no evidence of torture. Certainly she was severely abused, menaced, and malnourished. Survivors who were imprisoned with her attested that her fortitude and inextinguishable hope were inspirational.

Violette was incarcerated at Fresnes Prison south of the city, an immense, forbidding structure with 1,600 cells and dungeons in the basement. It was there that the SS housed captured SOE agents and members of the French Resistance. Periodically Violette was driven into Paris to be interrogated at the building on the avenue Foch—nicknamed the *"avenue Boche"* during the war—the incongruously lovely boulevard, lined with gardens and Second Empire mansions, that runs from the Arc de Triomphe to the Bois de Boulogne.

Violette endured seven weeks of this treatment. There is no sugges- tion that she gave up any useful information. The interrogators were done with her by the first week in August. On August 8 she was led to the prison yard, where three small coaches waited. Male prisoners were put into the first two, and female prisoners—about a dozen, including Violette—into the third. They were driven to the Gare de l'Est railroad station and put aboard a train bound for Germany.

The train was a short one, with several cars containing wounded German soldiers, a car carrying an antiaircraft gun, and, bringing up the rear, a prison car. This was divided into three compartments off a corridor. Two had their seats removed and were fitted with iron gates, like stalls for animals. The men were crammed into these, with no room to sit. The women were put into the third compartment, which had seats, and chained together by the ankles, in pairs. The car had a guard station and, for the guards, a lavatory.

The prisoners included several SOE agents besides Violette. Notable among these was Wing Commander Forest Yeo-Thomas, known to friends as Tommy, and to the Gestapo as "the White Rabbit" for his elusiveness. Famously brave, Yeo-Thomas had undertaken hair-raising missions in France for SOE's F Section—at one point having to conceal his identity from Klaus Barbie while the two took tea together in a railroad dining car—and had risen to the top of the Gestapo's most wanted list. Betrayed in Paris, he had been imprisoned at Fresnes and horribly tortured at avenue Foch. Now, as the ranking officer aboard, he took command of the prisoners on the train.

Late in the afternoon the train pulled out of the Gare de l'Est bound for Saarbrücken, just over the border in Germany. It crept slowly through the French countryside. When night fell, Yeo-Thomas arranged for the men to take turns lying down, four at a time, while the rest remained standing, as that was all the space permitted. The men had some bottles of water supplied by the Red Cross, but it was all gone by sunrise.

In the morning the heat grew stifling, and by afternoon it was unbearable. The men clamored for water, but the guards gave them none.

At around 2:00 P.M. the train was approaching Châlons-sur-Marne, about halfway to the German border, when a pair of RAF warplanes appeared overhead. They flew down low and released bombs. The front of the train erupted in a tremendous explosion. Seventeen Germans were killed. Glass shards from shattered windows flew in all directions. The train lurched to a stop.

As the airplanes banked to make another run, guards scampered off the train to take cover in fields, leaving their captives locked in the prison car. The guards took a machine gun with them and trained it on the carriage in case any prisoners tried to make a run for it. The train's antiaircraft gun began firing.

The RAF planes made another pass, flying very low. They dropped more bombs and strafed the train with machine-gun fire. The prisoners heard the screams of wounded and dying Germans. Already half crazed with thirst, the men locked in the stalls began to panic, fearing that they would be burned alive—the ammunition aboard British warplanes, they knew, frequently included incendiary rounds.

At that moment, Yeo-Thomas saw an astonishing sight: Violette, on knees and elbows, coming toward him, bearing water. As he told one of her biographers afterward: "We all felt deeply ashamed when we saw Violette Szabo, while the raid was still on, come crawling along the corridor towards us with a jug of water which she had filled in the lavatory. She handed it to us through the iron bars. With her, crawling too, came the girl to whose ankle she was chained."[1]

The two women took the empty jug and crawled back along the corridor for more water—over and over again. "My God, that girl had guts," Yeo-Thomas said.

The warplanes flew off, leaving the train a smoking ruin, unable to move. The guards transferred the prisoners to trucks requisitioned from nearby farms. They drove to Metz, where the prisoners spent the night in stables attached to the German barracks. Over the next several days they made their way to the frontier and crossed into Germany. On reaching Saarbrücken they were interned at an especially gruesome Gestapo facility called Neue Bremm, a transshipment depot for prisoners bound for concentration camps. Because it was a temporary holding area, the place had no heat, no proper shelter, and hardly any food for captives. Violette was held there, in a pen exposed to the weather, for ten days.

Violette and Yeo-Thomas parted ways at Neue Bremm. She was sent to Ravensbrück, the concentration camp for women; he was sent to Buchenwald. Yeo-Thomas had no expectation that he would survive Buchenwald. He was sent there in a group of thirty-six SOE and Resistance captives; not long after they arrived, sixteen of them were hanged in a basement. Yeo-Thomas, figuring that he would soon follow, wrote a farewell letter to his commander, Lieutenant Colonel Leonard Henry ("Dizzy") Dismore, in the hope that it might be smuggled out of the camp and delivered to Baker Street. It reads:

14 September 1944

My dear Dizzy,

These are "famous last words" I am afraid, but one has to face death one day or another so I will not moan and get down to brass tacks.

I will not attempt to make a report on my journey except to say that up to the very moment of my arrest it had been a success and I had got things cracking and woken up a number of slumberers. I was quite pleased with things—I took every precaution and neglected nothing—my capture was due to one of those incidents one cannot provide for—I had so much work that I was overwhelmed so I asked [a Free French commander] to provide me with a sure dependable agent de liaison, and he gave me a young chap called Guy, whom I renamed Antonin. He worked for me for a week, and then got caught; how I do not know, but in any case, he had an appointment with me at 11 A.M. on Tuesday 21st March at the Metro Passy [in Paris] and brought the Gestapo with him. He was obviously unable to withstand bullying and very quickly gave in to questioning. I was caught coming round a corner and had not an earthly chance, being collared and handcuffed before I could say "knife." I was badly beaten up in the car on the way to Gestapo H.Q., arriving there with a twisted nose and a head about twice its normal size.

I was then subjected to four days continuous grilling, being beaten up and also being put into a bath of icy cold water, legs and arms chained, and held head downwards under water until almost drowned, then pulled out and asked if I had anything to say. This I underwent six times but I managed to hold out and gave nothing away. Not a single arrest was made as a sequel to my capture. The only trouble was that the party who was lodging me got arrested and will have to be compensated for losing liberty and home. The name is Mlle. Sandoe, 11 rue Claude Chahu, Paris, 16eme. . . .

I was interrogated for about 2 months, but dodged everything. . . . I nearly lost my left arm as a result of the tortures, as I got blood poisoning through my wrist being cut to the bone by chains and remaining unattended with handcuffs biting into them for about 6 days. Apart from that I was kept in solitary confinement for 4 months at Fresnes. I was very unpopular as a Britisher, and one of the German N.C.O.'s. . . . was particularly glad at every opportunity of punching me or slapping my face. He gave me 3 weeks of glass-house [punitive confinement] in a darkened cell, without mattress, blankets, deprived of all means of washing, and with about a 1/2 pound of bread per day as sole food. I was pretty weak when I came out, had lost about 2 1/2 stone in weight. I was sent to [an internment camp at] Compiègne on

July 17th, whilst there recuperated a bit and had arranged an escape together with a chap. . . . whose name is Roberty, and got sent to Weimar on the eve of escaping. Roberty succeeded. Bad luck for me.

The journey here was an eventful one, it took 8 days. . . . We had various adventures, all were handcuffed the whole time, 19 men in one compartment and 18 in another. We could not move being packed in like sardines. The gates of the compartments were padlocked and we had very little air, no food had been provided for. We were given 1 day's rations which had to last 5 days, luckily some had Red Cross parcels or we would have starved. The train was bombed and machine-gunned on the way and we had a very narrow shave. Our escorts ran and left us helpless, had the train caught fire we would have burned like trapped rats. We had to stop at Saar-brücken for 3 days in a punishment and reprisals camp, and were beaten up on arrival. As usual I seemed to attract particular attention and got well and truly slapped and cuffed. We were confined for three days and nights, 37 of us in a hut 9 feet by 7 feet by 7 feet. It was Hell.

We then came on to this place Buchenwald. On the way our escorts plundered and stole practically all our effects. Never believe about German honesty, they are the biggest thieves, liars, bullies and cowards I have ever met. In addition, they delight in torturing people and gloat over it. Upon arrival which took place about midnight, we were locked up in the disinfection quarters and next morning we were nearly hanged summarily, but temporarily reprieved. We were stripped, completely shorn and dressed in prison rags, losing our few remaining belongings, and 16 of us. . . . were told to report to a certain place. We never saw them again and found out that they were being hung without trial on the night of 11/12 September. They have been cremated so no trace remains of them. We are now awaiting our turn. There are 170 airmen (British and American) brought down and captured in France, but they are being treated as Terror Fliers and sleeping in the open, living under appalling conditions in violation of all conventions. They ought to be treated as POW. Men die like flies here. . . . The bearer of this letter will give you all details so I will not say more—whatever he tells you is Gospel truth. He is no romancer, and he will never be able to really do justice to the horrors perpetrated here. Dizzy, see to it that our people never let ourselves be softened to the German people, or there will be another war in 15 years' time and all our lives will have been sacrificed in vain. I leave it to you and others to see that retribution is fierce. It will never be fierce enough.[2]

Yeo-Thomas's letter was smuggled out of Buchenwald, and for decades it lay buried in the SOE archive. The White Rabbit himself, though barely able to walk, contrived to escape from the concentration camp and make it back to London. In 1946 he was awarded the George Cross—the U.K.'s second-highest honor, after the Victoria Cross—for conspicuous bravery. He was one of six SOE agents to receive it.

Violette was also one of the six, although her George Cross had to be awarded posthumously. She arrived at Ravensbrück in early September 1944. Conditions were horrific. Violette made plans to escape, but before she could act on them she was sent to work in a munitions factory at Torgau, in eastern Germany, and then on to a slave-labor camp at Königsberg, south of Berlin, where conditions were even worse than at Ravensbrück. Food consisted of watery soup with a few vegetable peelings, and scraps of bread. As winter set in, Violette and the other female slaves, dressed in thin rags, were made to chop down trees and dig in frozen earth to level ground for a new runway. There was no heat in their barracks; at night the women huddled together on thin, vermin-infested palliasses to share their body warmth. Many were worked to death.

Toward the end of January 1945, Violette was returned to Ravensbrück. There, one evening, she and two friends—Denise Bloch and

Lilian Rolfe, also captured SOE agents—were taken to a spot between the camp's gas chambers known as Execution Alley. A German guard murdered each woman with a single shot to the back of the neck from a small-caliber pistol. According to witnesses, Violette was the last to be executed.

31

In the words of André Malraux: "It was a time when, out in the countryside, we listened tensely to the barking of dogs in the depths of the night; a time when multicolored parachutes, laden with weapons and cigarettes, fell from the sky by the light of flares burning in forest clearings or on windswept plateaus; a time of cellars, and the desperate cries of the torture victims, their voices like those of children. . . . The great battle in the darkness had begun."

Malraux was speaking at a ceremony in December 1964, recalling the fighting in France after D-Day. The occasion was the transfer of the ashes of Jean Moulin, the Resistance hero martyred by Klaus Barbie, to the Panthéon in Paris. Malraux was minister of culture at the time. Addressing Moulin's ghost, he went on:

"Poor tortured king of shadows, behold your people of shadows rise up in the June night. . . . Hear the roar of the German tanks, racing back towards Normandy, over the plaintive cries of sheep and cattle disturbed by their passing. . . . the tanks will arrive too late. And, Prefect, as the Allied breakthrough begins . . . behold your ragged tramps crawl from their oak maquis, laying their farmers' hands to bazookas to bring to a halt one of the finest armored divisions of Hitler's empire, the *Das Reich* division."[1]

———

A FEW ELEMENTS of *Das Reich* did make it as far as Normandy by the closing days of July 1944, but not in time to tip the balance of war. North of the Loire River the Allies had by then achieved complete air superiority—Operation Overlord wasn't just history's largest seaborne invasion, it was also the biggest aerial campaign the world had seen. Mustangs, Spitfires, Mosquitos, Thunderbolts, and other Allied warplanes flew an average of six hundred sorties a day over northern France, hunting enemy convoys with bombs, rockets, cannons, and machine-gun fire. The Germans generally could travel only by night, heavily camouflaged.

As August began, Allied tanks and troops broke out of the *bocage*. They marched southward into Brittany and southern Normandy, and then turned east. The drive to Paris, and on to Germany, was under way.

On August 15 a second invasion of France, called Operation Dragoon, began on the Mediterranean coast. Originally code-named Operation Anvil (as the Normandy invasion was originally code-named Sledgehammer), it is less well remembered than the D-Day landing, but it played a critical part in driving the Germans out of France and toppling the puppet Vichy regime. With Operation Dragoon the Allies secured the deepwater ports of Marseille and Toulon, and poured men and matériel ashore from troopships. The German Army Group B, overmatched, withdrew to the north and east through the Rhône Valley.

In the Limousin, in central France—between Sledgehammer and Anvil—it became clear that the momentum of the war was turning. The battle of Mont Gargan, and the rest of the German *ratissage,* had done some damage to Operation Salesman II. The Nazis had discovered and destroyed a couple of *maquis* encampments, and they had disrupted the guerrillas' telephone and food-distribution systems. By early August, though, the SS troops had mostly left the countryside and returned to Limoges, and the Salesman operation was back up to the strength it had reached before Bastille Day. Ambushes and sabotages resumed at a lively pace. More civilians, scenting victory, clamored to sign up. Dropping supplies fast enough to keep up with demand once again became a problem.

At the beginning of August, Baker Street sent the shock troops Philippe had been requesting. In a series of drops over five moonlit nights, eighteen OSS commandos parachuted into the Haute-Vienne. The team, led by Captain William F. Larson and code-named Percy Red, was the first Operational Group inserted into France.

Philippe, Jean Claude, and Bob received the men and escorted them to a large, isolated château Philippe had managed to requisition near La Croisille. The Salesman agents found that the OSS men possessed, as expected, unusual language proficiency; unfortunately, it was in Norwegian. Jean Claude never did find out why Norwegian speakers were sent to France. It didn't make much difference—they all spoke American English as well—except in the matter of coffee. They brought a lot of it, but they prepared it in the Norwegian manner, strong and black, which Jean Claude didn't like very much.

Two other men parachuted in with the OG, their arrival an additional sign that the tide of battle was turning. One was a "Dakota expert," Edgar Fraser, and the other was his wireless operator, Joseph Colette. "Dakota" was the British nickname for the Douglas C-47 transport plane, the military version of the legendary DC-3, better known in America as the "gooney bird." Fraser and Colette were sent to scout possible landing sites for the planes. The ability to have transports land and take off would of course be a huge logistical step up from moonlight parachute drops and furtive Lysander touch-and-go missions.

Jean Claude helped Colette make his first radio contacts with London, and then spent several days driving the two men around the

Haute-Vienne, Creuse, and Corrèze departments in search of likely airstrips. Near the town of Saint-Junien they came across an airfield that looked serviceable but needed improvement. Jean Claude left the men there and drove back to the château at La Croisille, where he found that the OG had wasted no time getting to work.

German troops had begun withdrawing to the northeast, toward home, where they could be expected to regroup. The OG men, alongside Salesman *maquisards,* set about making any movement out of Limoges as difficult as possible for the enemy, assaulting roads and rail lines and making most of them impassable. London assigned a high priority to the railway between Tours and Vierzon. During the first week in August, the OG commandos destroyed half a mile of rail, and a bridge, on that line. German troops attacked near Villechenoux to try to stop the sabotage; the OG men, in a furious counterattack, drove them off and inflicted heavy losses.

On August 10, Jean Claude was on ambush duty with the OGs on the main road out of Limoges when Philippe received a tip from informers at a railroad depot near Salon-la-Tour, where his men had piled up the two trains in June. The Germans had finally cleared enough of the debris to use one of the tracks, and were planning to send freight trains, accompanied by an armored train, from Limoges to Toulouse.

Philippe and Jean Claude quickly led the OGs to a spot a little way up the line from the Salon cut. They set up camouflaged charges and waited for the trains. By late afternoon it became obvious that the trains were not coming—the Germans had generally given up traveling after dark in the region by then—so they blew the charges and went home, disappointed.

The next day an informer brought the news that the trains were on the move. They had paused about six miles away to repair a bridge before proceeding. Another armored train, the agents learned, was on its way up from Brive, about thirty miles to the south, to assist.

That night Philippe led a group of *maquisards* and OG men back to the railroad line, to another deep cut near Salon. Jean Claude did not go with them, as he had reception duty and high-priority messages to transmit to London. The guerrillas placed charges and waited, hiding.

When the sun came up they saw that a concrete pylon, unnoticed in the dark, was tilted toward the tracks—no doubt a casualty of some previous act of sabotage. There was no time to straighten it, or to move the charges. At any rate, the men thought a German train would be able to squeeze past it.

An armored train came rumbling down the tracks and stopped at the pylon. German soldiers disembarked, some to repair the pylon, others to cover them while they worked. Philippe's men held their breath, hoping their explosive charges would not be discovered.

There was a shout—a German soldier spotted one of the guerrillas.

An intense firefight erupted. Philippe's men detonated the charges and retreated under heavy fire. Several of them were wounded. The OG's commander, Captain Larson, was killed.

The armored train and its convoy returned to Limoges. The second armored train, on the way from Brive, was stopped by a simple expedient: A *maquis* group blew up a cliffside at a narrow gorge, sending several hundred tons of rock onto the tracks and blocking them completely.

Captain Larson's body was recovered the next day. The Salesman agents gave Larson a full military burial. But as when they lost Violette, they had little time to mourn. By then Philippe was working on an ambitious new idea: the liberation of Limoges.

32

Limoges was a metropolis on edge. A gray manufacturing city built on the porcelain industry, it was populated in the summer of 1944 by occupiers, resisters, collaborators, and war-weary citizens, all sensing that some kind of endgame was at hand. Any thoughts of taking the city by force, though, were tempered by the memory of Tulle. If the SS had been capable of mass reprisals against noncombatants in that rural village, what horror might be provoked by a botched attack on the Limousin capital?

In fact, Guingouin had received an order, back in June, from a French Communist Party official to try to capture Limoges. He had refused, citing the Tulle massacre. Now, two months later, the city was still a heavily fortified bastion. German forces included fifteen hundred SS troops under the command of *Generalmajor* (Major General) Walter Gleininger, equipped with tanks and flamethrowers. There were also units of *Das Reich*, the Gestapo, and the Abwehr; and a large group of extremely nervous *Milice,* who anticipated, correctly, that their collaboration with the Nazis would come to a bad end.

Philippe, Jean Claude, Bob, and Guingouin drew up a plan to cut Limoges off from the surrounding countryside. It was easily accomplished—the airport was useless, as the Germans had sliced deep trenches through the runways, and train and road traffic were at a near standstill from previous demolitions. Jean Claude and Bob were assigned to lead ambush teams at key approaches to the city, tightening the cordon established by the OGs. A German attempt to get through a roadblock on the Limoges-Montauban road was for the most part frustrated over a three-day period, leaving some hundred dead and many wounded. The *Milice* tried a breakout northeastward toward Grandmont, and they too were forced back.

Guingouin sent leaflets into Limoges calling for a general strike, and urging the Vichy police to join the Resistance. He also had raiding parties probe the city's outskirts. Philippe held meetings with the heads of *maquis* factions, and it was agreed that Guingouin would henceforth be recognized as the regional leader of the FFI, the Resistance umbrella organization.

On the morning of August 20, a Sunday, Philippe and Jean Claude made contact with Jean d'Albis, the Swiss chargé d'affaires in Limoges, asking whether he would be willing to act as a neutral intermediary in a negotiation with Gleininger. By noon the arrangements were made, and d'Albis presented Gleininger with the guerrillas' terms of capitulation: unconditional surrender, with formal prisoner status given to his troops. Gleininger refused, saying that he would deal only with the Vichy government, not with irregulars.

That afternoon Philippe sent revised terms in writing, via d'Albis, to Gleininger. They stipulated that the surrender would be to Anglo-Franco-American troops; that surrendering soldiers would be interned in a camp with special quarters for officers; that conditions for prisoners would be the same as those for Allied troops interned in Germany; and that wounded men would be left to recuperate in hospitals under Allied medical supervision. Philippe also proposed that, as a symbolic gesture, the general himself would not be disarmed. Gleininger agreed to provide safe passage for Philippe's team to meet for talks at d'Albis' residence in Limoges the following day.

That evening Philippe briefed Jean Claude on the discussions. Jean Claude was momentarily thrilled when Philippe told him, half in jest, that he might be called on to represent the United States in treaty negotiations with the German general. It was not to be, however. At the last minute a U.S. Army captain was located, a commando who had recently parachuted in, and as he outranked Jean Claude he was deemed a more suitable representative. Philippe would represent England, and a pair of *maquis* commanders would represent France.

The next afternoon Jean Claude watched Philippe's delegation drive off toward Limoges in two Citroëns, one flying French and English flags, the other French and American flags. The cars pulled up at d'Albis' residence at 4:00 P.M. Gleininger's party arrived at the same time, and there was a brief contretemps over who should go through the door first, until it was decided that all parties would enter in order of rank.

Gleininger began by stating categorically that he was not ready to surrender, and asked: Why should he? Philippe replied that the day before, immediately after Gleininger had agreed to negotiate, he had called off a massive Allied aerial bombardment of the city. Further, he had suspended operations by twenty thousand FFI guerrillas under his command who, at that moment, encircled Limoges. He also said that U.S. armored columns were advancing toward the city, making immediate surrender necessary to avoid civilian bloodshed.

None of this was true. But it prompted Gleininger to ask another question: What would happen if he refused?

Philippe replied that he would attack. He said it was doubtful that he, or anyone else, would be able to control the "rebel FFI"—he used the Germans' own epithet for the *maquisards*—and that he believed there would be no German prisoners taken alive. Guingouin and his men, he said, were barbarous killers.

Gleininger requested a break in the meeting to discuss matters with his staff. At 5:15, discussions resumed with a statement from the general: "Gentlemen, I accept your proposals."

The talks then turned to the logistics of surrender. It was agreed that FFI forces would enter Limoges by the Toulouse road, and that a German officer from each barrack would be present to escort them. The treaty would not cover anyone offering any resistance. All weapons were to be deposited in the barracks' yards. The surrendering troops would march fourteen miles to an internment camp at Saint-Paul; anyone over age forty-five would have to walk only partway, and would then be transported by vehicle. Officers would be imprisoned in a château.

The signing of the surrender, it was agreed, would take place that evening at 8:00, at Gleininger's headquarters in Limoges.

In fact, when the Allied delegation arrived at the German headquarters there was no sign of General Gleininger. A German captain there informed them that one of the general's superior officers in Lyon had gotten wind of his agreement to surrender, and had countermanded it. SS troops had kidnapped Gleininger and were breaking out of the city. Meanwhile, in Limoges Centre, occupiers of different factions—Gestapo, regular army, and SS—were fighting one another. As a Baker Street daily report put it:

> 22nd August. Hamlet [a code name for Philippe] reported that Limoges was ours after successful negotiations during which orders from Lyon arrived to refuse surrender. The result was a fantastic muddle in which the Germans happily shot each other, while most of the remainder tried to break through towards Lyon. General Gleininger was arrested by the Gestapo after signing surrender to Hamlet and is reputed to have committed suicide.

In the confusion, Philippe sent in FFI fighters to attack the German barracks. The Limoges police switched sides, as Guingouin had urged, and helped the guerrillas take the city block by block. Philippe,

Jean Claude (*left*) and Philippe (*right, foreground*)
in liberated Limoges in August 1944, outside the former
Gestapo headquarters they took over for their billet.

the wily student of politics trained at Sciences-Po, had managed to capture Limoges by bluff. It was the first major city in France to be liberated by the Resistance without the help of regular Allied troops.

Jean Claude didn't enter Limoges right away; he and Bob each led an ambush team to try to contain the German breakout toward Lyon. The guerrillas couldn't stop the German troops and armor completely— they had no weapons heavier than bazookas—but they inflicted serious casualties, took several hundred prisoners, destroyed a good deal of equipment, and slowed the enemy down considerably.

When Jean Claude arrived in Limoges three days after the negotiations fell apart, he found that the gunfire had mostly ceased, and the wave of bloody retribution which almost invariably followed the liberation of cities and towns—called the *épuration sauvage,* or "wild purge"—had begun. Perhaps the most enduring image of these paroxysms is that of bald French women frog-marched through the streets— women who, accused of having slept with Germans, had their hair shorn off to broadcast their shame. But the score settling could be far worse.

In Limoges, tribunals were set up to try, judge, and sentence people who had collaborated with, or in some other way aided, the occupiers and the Vichy regime. No appeals were permitted, and punishment was immediate. Over just a few days, the tribunals handled some 350 cases. Seventy-five people were sentenced to death—45 of them by a tribunal headed by Guingouin—and many others to long prison terms or forced labor. One person who came before a tribunal, Jean Claude learned many years later, was the jailer who had promised to "look after" Violette in her captivity, taking payments from the Salesman agents even after she had been moved out of Limoges. The man was tried and executed, along with his entire family.

Alongside the savagery, of course, there was jubilation. It made for an exceedingly bizarre atmosphere that Jean Claude never forgot.

There would be public executions taking place in one street, and an uproarious block party going on in the next.

The strange dissonance extended to Jean Claude's billet. He was lodged, with Philippe and Bob, in an ornate town house in the rue Louvrier de Lajolais—the very building that the Gestapo had used for its headquarters. It was there that Violette had been taken for interrogation after her capture at Salon-la-Tour. The town house was extravagantly comfortable, with a large drawing room, a bar, a formal dining room, and bathrooms with hot water. Two women served as cooks and housekeepers. Happy crowds gathered when the Salesman agents stepped out the door.

Jean Claude took a room on the top floor, where wireless reception was best. It wasn't really necessary, though, as operational radio traffic with London had slowed to a trickle. The Salesman agents spent the closing days of August helping to restore order in the city. Fraser, the Dakota expert, quickly had the Limoges airport repaired and running. Great quantities of troops and supplies were flown in. Prisoners freed from German captivity, including a group of twenty-four downed U.S. airmen, were flown out for home.

33

In the short term, the liberation of Limoges actually amplified the peril faced by Jean Claude, Philippe, and Bob. The Germans were on the move now, and in the countryside. Throughout southwestern France, occupying troops retreated before the pressure of the Allied Mediterranean invasion. Many moved homeward through the Salesman territory—up from Bordeaux to Angoulême, and then on toward Poitiers—some in orderly troop movements, others in panicked flight. The brutality of the occupation had left Frenchmen in a vengeful spirit, and Nazi soldiers felt that if they had to surrender, it was safest to do so to American or British troops. When they stumbled across bands of *maquisards* they fought furiously, afraid that capture would mean summary execution.

The Salesman agents led raiding parties out of Limoges to harry the Germans and clear out remaining enemy strongpoints. Jean Claude was more or less freed from his radio duties—other wireless operators had been flown in, and besides, the fighting was so fluid that there was little use for direction from London.

Philippe received a report that Germans had taken over a big château near Châteauroux, northeast of Limoges, and were using it to shelter troops and coordinate their retreat. With Jean Claude and Bob, he rounded up a large group of *maquisards* and led them to the château. There were a few skirmishes, and one intense firefight, and then the Germans withdrew.

Philippe, Jean Claude, and Bob were enjoying a brief moment of celebration when an Allied bomber, a Martin B-26 Marauder, flew down low and fast over the château. Passing right over their heads, the big twin-engine plane was hit by enemy ground fire. Jean Claude watched in horror as the left wing exploded off the fuselage. The flaming bomber crashed a short distance away.

Jean Claude, Philippe, and some of the *maquisards* hustled over to the wreckage to see if there were any survivors. They found none. They heard a short burst of gunfire in the distance, but gunshots were so routine by then that they paid no particular attention.

As they regrouped to leave the crash site, they realized that Bob was not with them. They went back to the château and searched it room by room, but they found no sign of him. Someone said he had been seen going alone toward a road at the foot of a slope beyond the château. They searched up and down the road, without success. Bob was gone.

Jean Claude and Philippe, dispirited, returned to Limoges.

As the fighting began to subside, Philippe was kept busy coordinating the restoration of order in the city. Jean Claude, having relatively little to do, brooded. With half the Salesman team now gone, their old theme song, "I'll Be Around," was sadly inapt.

One evening about two weeks later, Jean Claude was alone in the luxurious Limoges town house when the phone rang. It was Bob. In a perfectly natural tone, as if he were asking a small favor, Bob inquired whether someone might be able to pick him up in Moulins, at the Café de la République.

Jean Claude ran to find Philippe. The two men borrowed a car and took off through the rainy night for Moulins, 140 miles to the east. Philippe drove so fast that Jean Claude feared for his life, but the old racer's reflexes were still sharp and they made excellent time, though they had to keep stopping at checkpoints.

They found Bob waiting in the café. He got into the car and they headed straight back for Limoges, at a saner pace. On the way, Bob told his story.

When the B-26 had crashed, and the others had gone off to the wreckage, Bob had thought it prudent to walk down to the roadside behind the château to check it for traffic. Coming over the crest of a hill, to his delight, were two or three helmeted Germans pushing bicycles, backlit by the setting sun. Bob stepped into the road, holding a Marlin submachine gun casually, and said, "Hands up, gentlemen, if you please." They gave him a curious look, but complied.

Just then Bob saw, cresting the hill behind his captives, an entire German convoy. There was a brief burst of fire—the shooting Jean Claude had heard from the crash site—and Bob was wounded slightly in the arm and taken prisoner. He was wearing a British uniform, and that probably saved his life. If the Germans had known he was an irregular, they would likely have killed him on the spot.

Instead, Bob was tied up and placed in the bed of a small truck, jammed between two fifty-gallon drums of gasoline and some artillery shells. The convoy continued on its way.

Bob was treated reasonably well—he was interrogated only in a cursory manner, and he ate the same food his captors did. He learned firsthand how demoralizing *maquis* ambushes—the kind he had so often led himself—could be. The convoy was continually attacked and delayed over several days as it pushed eastward. Casualties began to add up. Bob had visions of being trapped in an inferno if the gasoline drums on either side of him were hit and burst into flames.

As the convoy approached Moulins it passed through some particularly heavy ambushes. The German officer in charge realized that he had too many wounded men to care for, and that trying to transport them all would hinder the convoy's chances of making it the rest of the way to Germany. He offered Bob his freedom if, as a British officer, he would undertake to arrange for the wounded soldiers' care, safety, and formal surrender to the FFI. Bob very happily accepted. The German commander asked for Bob's word of honor as a British officer and an English gentleman. Bob solemnly gave it, without disclosing that he was neither.

The convoy was split in two. The soldiers who were still in fighting shape pressed on for Germany. Bob took charge of the rest, and led them, under a white flag, into Moulins. There he transferred them to the care of nuns and local FFI commanders. Then he went to the Café de la République and telephoned Limoges for a ride.

34

By mid-September the tribunals had done their work in Limoges, and order was largely restored. The FFI decided to mark the city's liberation with a *prise d'armes,* a military review.

Companies of *maquisards* paraded through the city, dressed for once in snappy uniforms—Jean Claude never did find out how they had been provided so quickly—and wearing FFI armbands emblazoned with the double-barred Cross of Lorraine, the Free French riposte to the swastika. They passed in review before a committee of FFI commanders and city officials, and formed up in ranks.

Jean Claude, Philippe, and Bob stood in a line before the committee, in uniform. Jean Claude wore his tall paratroop boots. Each agent was presented with a Croix de Guerre with a red-and-green ribbon, a medal for heroism in combat bestowed by de Gaulle's government in exile. In addition, Jean Claude received from Guingouin a rare French Resistance Croix de Guerre, with a bronze star and a white-and-gold ribbon. Jean Claude was moved—it was the first and only time he was decorated in public. He received many other medals in his subsequent career, including a Silver Star from the U.S. government, but all were for classified work, bestowed in private ceremonies.

The war had moved on, toward the German frontier. Allied troops

Jean Claude receiving the Croix de Guerre at a ceremony in Limoges.
Philippe Liewer and Bob Maloubier are fourth and fifth from the left.
Behind Jean Claude, wearing a beret and glasses, is Georges Guingouin.

had liberated Paris in late August. Philippe received orders from Baker Street to begin closing down Operation Salesman II—it was only then that Jean Claude learned the operation's name.

Jean Claude requested permission to attempt a trip to Conliège in the Jura—far to the east, near the border with Switzerland, where fighting still raged—to check on *Grandmère*. Somewhat to his surprise, he was granted a travel pass and a ten-day leave. He realized that he would be traveling on many of the same roads that he and his brother Pierre had taken, in the other direction, when they had fled toward Portugal before the Nazi invasion in May 1940. He had departed Conliège as a scared French high-school student. He headed back a remarkably changed man—a trained killer, a secret agent, a U.S. citizen, a decorated combat veteran—though still just twenty years old.

Jean Claude borrowed a car and left Limoges with some advance pay to give *Grandmère* so that she could afford black-market prices. It was slow going, as Jean Claude was frequently held up at FFI checkpoints. Guards were suspicious of a French-speaking American, with seemingly official French government passes, driving alone toward the battlefront.

As Jean Claude progressed farther east he was warned of heavy fighting ahead. The sound of gunfire grew constant. Finally, near Chalon-sur-Saône, about forty miles short of Conliège, he was forbidden to go on. He considered proceeding by back roads, but by then the sounds of battle nearly surrounded him. Reluctantly, he packed his cash, some chocolate, and a note to *Grandmère* into a small parcel and trusted it to the local post office. It was a gamble, he knew. *Grandmère* never received it.

Arriving back in Limoges, Jean Claude found that Philippe was nearly done wrapping up Operation Salesman II. On September 22, the agents decided to head for Paris. Jean Claude, Philippe, and Bob left for the freshly liberated capital in high style. In the garage of a château, they found a gleaming Hispano-Suiza, a luxury touring car with a long hood, exquisite coachwork, and a convertible top. In the château's *cave*, they came across a large supply of plum brandy. They requisitioned both, leaving a handwritten note declaring that it was a military necessity.

The drive to Paris was slow but festive. When they ran low on gas, they nursed the car along by drizzling brandy into the tank—suitably refined fuel for such a regal vehicle, perhaps, but not entirely to the big engine's liking. The problem was solved when they came across a stopped U.S. Army truck, whose driver gladly traded them three jerry cans of gasoline for one of several German Iron Crosses they carried as souvenirs.

When the agents arrived in Paris, the city was in a delirium of celebration. They found a very expensive black-market restaurant, parked the car outside, and went in for a long, glorious lunch.

When they emerged hours later, the Hispano-Suiza was gone. Their stolen car had been stolen.

Jean Claude looked at Philippe and Bob, and shrugged.

"Fortunes of war," he said.

Jean Claude and Bob at the opening of the Violette Szabo Museum
on June 24, 2000. It was their first reunion after fifty-six years.

EPILOGUE

Georges Guingouin was elected mayor of Limoges in 1945. He fell out of favor with the French Communist Party, however, possibly because many party officials who outranked him had less illustrious careers in the Resistance. He was expelled from the party in November 1952.

As the Cold War settled in, a segment of France's population turned against former Communist resisters. In December 1953, Guingouin was arrested for crimes allegedly committed at the liberation. In February 1954, he survived an attempt to murder him in prison. He was released in June, and former resisters rallied to his cause. He was finally absolved of blame in 1959. He returned to teaching and lived a quiet life until he died in 2005, at age ninety-two.

HEINZ LAMMERDING, commander of the *Das Reich* division, survived the war and went home to what became West Germany after the country's partition. In 1953 he was tried in absentia for war crimes in France, and sentenced to death for the massacres at Tulle and Oradour-sur-Glane. West German authorities refused to extradite him. He lived in freedom, working as a building contractor, until his death in 1971, at age sixty-five.

Aurel Kowatsch, the officer in charge of the SS troops in Tulle, died in March 1945 in fighting on the eastern front. Adolf Diekmann, in charge of the troops at Oradour, was killed in action weeks after the massacre there.

Oradour was never rebuilt. The French government decided that its remains should be preserved "in a ruined state," and so they endure today, as a memorial to the victims and a reminder of the Nazi occupation's brutality.

LEO MARKS'S POEM "The Life That I Have" was never intended for publication. But when the British producer Daniel Angel made a movie about Violette Szabo's life, called *Carve Her Name with Pride*—based on the biography of the same title by R. J. Minney—he asked Marks's permission to use the poem in the film. Marks assented, on the condition that his authorship not be revealed.

After the movie was released in 1958, the studio received thousands of letters asking who had written the poem. The studio remained mum, but it felt obligated to forward to Marks a letter from the father of an eight-year-old boy who was dying of cancer. The father enclosed a note from the boy, written in a simple code, and asked if someone could please reply.

Marks broke the code and read: "Dear code-master. She was very brave. Please how does the poem work. I'm going to be a spy when I grow up." Marks sent a reply, in the boy's own code, saying that he would happily explain the poem code to him just as soon as he was better. He enclosed the chess set that Violette had given him, saying he was sure she would have wanted the boy to have it. Six weeks later Marks received another letter from the father, saying that the boy had rallied, then died with the poem and the chess set on his bed.

Marks eventually published the poem in 1999, in a little booklet illustrated by his wife, Elena Gaussen Marks.

VIOLETTE SZABO'S BODY was never found. Witnesses said that her executioners tossed it into the crematorium at Ravensbrück.

After the war, a formidable SOE officer named Vera Atkins took it upon herself to travel to Europe and investigate the fates of all F Section agents who had gone missing. She obtained a statement from a Ravensbrück guard confirming the murders of Violette and her friends, Denise Bloch and Lilian Rolfe.

Once her death was verified, Violette was awarded the George Cross for bravery in 1946. In a private ceremony at Buckingham Palace, King George VI gave the medal to Violette's daughter Tania, then four years old. Tania wore the dress her mother had bought for her in Paris on her first Salesman mission.

AT BUCKINGHAM PALACE, when the brief investiture ceremony was done, a man walked out of the shadows in the rear of the room. He told Tania that her mother was a very brave, heroic woman. It was Philippe Liewer.

Little else is known about Liewer's brief life after the war. He settled in Casablanca, Morocco. He died there in 1948, of a heart attack, at age thirty-seven.

BOB MALOUBIER, at the conclusion of Operation Salesman II, joined SOE's Force 136, an elite commando group aiding resistance groups in Southeast Asian territories occupied by Japan. He endured a difficult campaign in Laos, where guerrillas under his command were ambushed by both Chinese and Viet forces. His old *maquisard* companion Jacques Dufour—the man who had driven Violette to Salon-la-Tour on the day she was captured—died slowly in his arms. At one point his

The George Cross awarded to Violette Szabo was presented by King George
VI to her four-year-old daughter, Tania, in a private investiture at Buckingham
Palace on January 28, 1947. Tania wore the dress her mother bought for
her in the heart of occupied Paris on her first mission.

men came under frequent attacks from civilians. Bob discovered evidence that three local tax collectors were actually enemy agents. He had them killed, and the attacks ceased.

Bob returned to France in August 1946. He spent the next thirteen years with the newly formed *Service de Documentation Extérieure et de Contre-Espionnage* (SDECE). He formed a frogman unit that was so successful in training demonstrations against the French navy that the navy took it over. In 1953 he worked with the Swiss watchmaker Blancpain to develop the Fifty Fathoms watch, the first modern dive watch. As he wrote: "Our project . . . imagined a watch with a black dial, large numerals and clear indications using triangles, circles and squares, as well as an exterior rotating bezel mirroring the markers of the dial. We wanted at the beginning of a dive to position the bezel opposite the minute hand so as to be able to read the elapsed time. We wanted in effect that each of the markers be as clear as a guiding star for a shepherd."

At the height of the Cold War Bob was sent by the SDECE to Austria, assigned to identify which targets—tunnels, dams, power plants, bridges—should be blown up to immobilize the country in the event of a Soviet invasion. He then established a recruitment program and a training school for Central Europeans, infiltrating them as spies into the USSR and running their operations.

Bob's final French government intelligence assignment involved overseeing assassinations of North African leaders in revolt against France. During this period he and the SDECE became entangled with organized crime. At one particularly dangerous time Bob was being hunted by the French Mafia; the *Unione Corse,* or Corsican Mafia; and Israel's Mossad intelligence service, all at once. His boss instructed him to disappear—with full salary—in Montevideo, Uruguay, until things cleared up. Doubting that French Intelligence would be able to ensure his safety, Bob took off in his Cessna and flew to Léopoldville, Congo, instead. Ordered back to France, he quit the intelligence service.

Bob found a job running lumber camps deep in the jungles of the Congo. He set up and ran a security force for that country's first prime minister, Léon M'ba. He worked for French oil companies in North Africa and the Mideast. It's safe to say that not all of Bob's professional activities were as morally unambiguous as his work with SOE in France during the war.

Bob returned to Paris in the early 1980s. He wrote several colorful books about his adventures, and was cast in a small role in a movie by Jean-Luc Godard, *Film Socialisme,* released in 2010. On June 5, 2014, the day before the seventieth anniversary of D-Day, he was made a Member of the Order of the British Empire by Queen Elizabeth II. He died the following year, of pancreatic cancer, at age ninety-two.

JEAN CLAUDE GUIET enjoyed a few giddy days of dining, drinking, and dancing in Paris after the Hispano-Suiza was stolen. Military policemen patrolled the city looking for deserters and spies, and Jean Claude—a twenty-year-old man in civilian clothing—was stopped and questioned several times. He dodged arrest with the help of his two sets of papers, but when he was stopped by a joint French-American patrol, the jig was up. Unwilling to risk being considered AWOL, which carried substantial penalties, Jean Claude produced both sets of documents and tried to explain himself. The MPs took him to their headquarters to figure out who he really was.

In short order, an older Englishman, also wearing civilian clothes, hurried in. Whatever papers he presented had an immediate impact, and Jean Claude was released into the man's custody. Accompanied by two French MPs, they went to Jean Claude's lodgings, where Jean Claude packed up his things and said a hurried good-bye to Bob. It would be fifty-six years before they met again. Jean Claude didn't have a chance to say good-bye to Philippe, who was out. They never saw each other again.

Jean Claude's escort put him on a crowded C-47 for a flight to London. Jean Claude didn't find out who the man was, but he recalled his words: "Well, whoever you are, SOE Baker Street was very happy to make your acquaintance again and especially relieved to learn that you had survived."

After a long debriefing at Franklin House, SOE gave Jean Claude a choice. He could parachute into Berlin, pose as a captured French slave laborer, and blow up factories until the Nazis surrendered. Or he could go home to Massachusetts, take four weeks' leave over Christmas, ship out for OSS jungle survival training on Catalina Island in California, and then go fight the Japanese in China and Burma. He picked the second option.

Jean Claude was sent home in a private first-class cabin aboard the *Queen Mary*. He reunited with his parents in Northampton, and spent his leave with them there. On the day after Christmas 1944, he went to Washington, D.C., where he joined a group of seven other OSS veterans for a cross-country train journey—in a boxcar with a toilet and a wood-burning stove—to Catalina Island.

Once their jungle training was complete, the agents traveled to Miami and boarded a C-47 for an epic flight to China. The plane stopped to refuel in more than twenty locations—including British Guiana, Belem, Ascension Island, Accra, El Fasher, Aden, Karachi, Agra, Colombo, Khandy, and Calcutta—before finally arriving in Hsian, China.

Jean Claude's experience in China and Burma was harsh and dark, and much of what he did there remains classified. He was attached to OSS Detachment 101, fighting behind enemy lines in Burma. According to U.S. government records, Detachment 101 was astonishingly

(BURMESE)

(CHINESE)

(SGAW KAREN)

(S. SHAN)

(W. SHAN)

17860

One of the silk squares issued to Jean Claude—known as a
blood chit—with messages asking for help in several languages.
The exact translation of the Chinese message reads:
Dear Respected Soldiers, Civilians, and Friends of Greater China,
We are American Air Force coming to China to assist in fighting against the
Japanese. Please provide assistance and rescue and please report to the nearby
Allies. The US government will definitely thank and reward you!
Great American China-Aiding Air Force
No. 17860.

effective: The unit killed 5,428 Japanese soldiers and rescued 574 Allied personnel, while losing only 22 Americans. In China Jean Claude fought with Group 10 and Team Ibex, part of an OSS effort to use Chinese troops in guerrilla operations against the Japanese occupiers.

Jean Claude often lived with local tribes deep in the jungle. He learned several dialects, though he lamented later that he had been unable to master the clicking sounds that some of them called for. Survival was made complex by enemy troops, local bandits, bloodsucking slugs, scorpions, and tigers. China was politically treacherous too. Jealousy, competition for funds, bureaucratic complexities on the ground, and unclear direction from Washington led to power struggles between the OSS and the U.S. Army. One day Jean Claude, emerging from the Chinese jungle after a particularly difficult operation, was ordered to report to OSS headquarters in Hsian. He was informed that he was up for two counts of court-martial, and that Army MPs were on their way to arrest him. He was charged with mailing letters in a foreign language, which was against regulations. Jean Claude had written two letters in French. One was to *Grandmère*—French was the only language she knew. The other was to Bob, and in that letter Jean Claude had criticized the treatment of Chinese Nationalist troops by their officers, violating a rule against disparaging allies.

The OSS headquarters staff in Hsian had been informed of the charges before Jean Claude emerged from the jungle, and had contacted Wild Bill Donovan. Donovan had recommended that Jean Claude make himself "unavailable" until the charges could be resolved. Told of this, Jean Claude grabbed his pack, carbine, ammunition, an extra canteen, and a sleeping bag, and hurried to the motor pool, where he found a large army truck and climbed in—not realizing that there was a howitzer attached to its trailer hitch. He joined a small convoy just leaving for Chengdu, and struggled to keep the truck on the rough road for what turned into a 1,100-mile drive.

Arriving in Chengdu, he was informed that the court-martial charges had been reduced to a fine—$88—and that he was being sent out of the Pacific theater. Within an hour he was loaded into a plane for Calcutta. There he caught a freighter down the Hooghly River to begin a three-month voyage back to the United States.

Discharged from the OSS, he went back to Harvard and graduated eighteen months later. He renewed his acquaintance with a beautiful young woman he had met during his freshman year, Gertrude Alice Flaherty, who was a part-time student at Boston University. They married in Cambridge, Massachusetts, in 1948. Jean Claude's parents disapproved of the union—they thought Gertrude, having grown up poor in North Adams, Massachusetts, a hardscrabble mill town, was an unsuitable match for their son—and did not attend the ceremony. Jean Claude's brother, Pierre, served as best man.

Jean Claude obtained a professorship at Ohio State and worked toward a Ph.D., but his insistence on flunking all his students was too much for the university, and his contract was not renewed. He went to work for the CIA.

The records of Jean Claude's career as a cold warrior remain classified. He undertook clandestine operations in Asia, the South Pacific, and elsewhere. The work meant uprooting his family frequently; Gertrude, their daughter, Claudia, and their son, Dan, coauthor of this volume, usually traveled with him. It appears that he left government service in the early 1960s. The family settled in Denver, and Jean Claude spent the remainder of his career ostensibly working at aerospace and defense contractors, including Melpar, Martin Marietta, and Honeywell. He never said much about what he did for them.

Jean Claude was a proud, discreet, highly trained agent, but in some important respects he did not fit the profile of a Cold War operative. He was an ardent supporter of the civil rights movement, having fought alongside many nonwhite Americans. He spoke up for immigrants, having served with many in the OSS (and of course he was an immigrant himself). He favored equal rights for women, having gone to battle with strong, capable women in the most challenging conditions.

Gertrude and Jean Claude were activists in the anti–Vietnam War movement from its earliest days. They worked with the American Friends Service Committee and the Unitarian Church to organize protests. Routinely, at demonstrations, men with short-cropped hair, dressed in sport jackets and ties, would walk up to Jean Claude, stop a few feet away, and take his photograph. It was assumed that they were from the FBI.

Gertrude and Jean Claude's home in Denver became something of a refuge for antiwar activists. When Jane Fonda gave a speech in Denver in 1970, they put her up for the night. They also provided lodging, food, cash, and transportation for eighteen-year-olds fleeing the draft en route to Canada. Once a month they hosted Mary Simmons, a Minnesota woman whose son, Pete, was serving time in a Colorado prison. He was one of the Minnesota 8, a group of war protesters who had broken into Selective Service offices and destroyed draft records. Whenever he was asked about his ardent opposition to the war in Vietnam, Jean Claude would say, "I was there and I know the truth. Our government is lying to its people about Vietnam and our boys are dying needlessly."

Jean Claude died in 2013, at home, a week after his eighty-ninth birthday.

AFTERWORD

DANIEL C. GUIET

I first cried for my father's passing the moment that I knew his journey was complete. It was four months after his death.

As we had been doing for years, my wife, Carol, and I had returned to the Jura, in eastern France, to spend time at our home, located just minutes from the house where Jean Claude had spent childhood summers with *Grandmère*. Dad was a quiet, self-contained, and in some ways mysterious man, but he always seemed to soften when he recalled the serene times he spent among the Conliège villagers before the Nazi invasion.

That July early morning was already hot. The deep blue sky was dotted by low-hanging cotton-ball clouds, creating the impression of a ceiling over the wide, vibrantly green pastures surrounding the town. The fields were bordered by high, nearly vertical rock ridges.

We drove up rue Haute, the narrow main street of Conliège. Towering row houses built within a foot of the curb, with front doors opening virtually into the street, blocked the sun. We squeezed past a few villagers carrying baguettes home from the tiny patisserie.

Turning left up a short, steep, seldom-used dirt path, we climbed to the Belvedere, a spot with a commanding view, a natural terrace held in place by a large rock retaining wall cut into the face of the steep hillside. The terrace was bordered by a rusting single iron rail mounted on its outer edge to prevent a misstep. The village lay below; we could see *Grandmère's* large home near its center. In the distance, church bells chimed softly, eight times.

Just above us was the Chapel of Sainte-Anne—an old, stone, single-story structure—and, adjacent to it, a small stone building known as the Hermitage. In centuries past it had been inhabited by a lookout, meagerly supported by the village, who lived practically as a hermit. He kept watch over the herds in the meadows below, and sounded an alarm in the event of approaching strangers, or fire. Looking southwest the sharp canyon opened, softening into an expansive plain that sloped gently down to the Ain River.

Leaning gently on the iron rail, we located a spot on the outer edge of the terrace that permitted a look down into the large courtyard of *Grandmère's* home. It was easy to locate Dad's bedroom window, and to imagine him as a child looking up from it at the prominent Belvedere. We could see the massive wooden gates that provided access to the large courtyard and out through the back to the pastureland behind the house.

Above and below us birds glided by. Carol and I hugged. I began tearing up as I leaned over the rail—although I had to smile as I caught myself automatically checking the direction of the light breeze, a reflex handed down from my father, who taught me to sail. Jean Claude was a loving, kind, and attentive man. He had a quick wit and loved reading. He always kept a small vegetable garden no matter where we lived, and it never had any dandelions in it—Jean Claude found that his Fairbairn-Sykes dagger was just the right length for slicing their roots, four inches down, before lifting them out of the soil.

Jean Claude was quick to laugh, with an easy smile that triggered a large happy dimple—the movies of Laurel and Hardy, the Marx Brothers, and W. C. Fields regularly brought him to tears of laughter. Quietly introspective, a superbly gifted linguist, understated in all things, he cherished being American but always carried with him a modesty and politeness that grew from his formal upbringing and French roots.

I slowly emptied a small container of his ashes into the breeze. The light gray cloud blew perhaps twenty feet across the hillside and fell onto a patch of purple wildflowers. The flowers will be there every summer.

Carol and I held each other and wept. Dad was home. It was July 14, 2013—Bastille Day.

THE LAST SURVIVOR

I n 2017, as this book was being researched, I was put in touch with
James Edgar, one of three living SOE F Section agents. Like my father,
James was a wireless operator. He parachuted into France on the night of
July 8, 1944, as a member of the Tilleul team, a circuit adjacent to the
Salesman II territory. Jean Claude led the reception committee that met
him at the drop zone. James wrote me a letter describing the experience.

Before joining the Tilleul circuit, James had taken part in Operation
Basalt in October 1942, one of the first SOE missions of the war. It was
a raid on the Nazi-occupied island of Sark in the English Channel. The
mission gained valuable intelligence, sent a message to the enemy that
England was probing the Continent, and prompted Hitler to issue the
so-called Commando Order, which directed that any Allied commandos
found in Europe or Africa should be executed on the spot, without a trial,
even if they were in uniform or tried to surrender.

James's SOE records remain classified through January 2021.

6 March 2017

Dear Dan,

A few lines to say how delighted I am that we are now in touch.
Although I am now 97 years old and that it was 73 years ago that I

met your father Jean Claude, in Sussac, I remember it well. Those
were momentous days.

I know that SOE radio operators had a very short life expectancy—
in the summer of 1944 we considered anything over 3 weeks' survival
in occupied France as a life well done. So your father very much put
his life on the line. I know Liewer was a very good agent and experienced leader and was very sensible to ignore some of London's stupid
orders. Actually a wonder that SOE achieved what it did, in spite of
horrible losses. I have always thought the Circuit Tilleul went in too
late and should have been at least 3 weeks earlier since much of the
intense action was over by the time we arrived. However we did our bit.

The Tilleul mission left for France on the night of 8th July 1944.
I'd been driven up from London to the American air base at Harrington in Northamptonshire with six other members of the group. I
now know that the crew of our B-24 Liberator were the renowned
"Carpetbaggers." Our group was to fly out in two planes a few minutes
apart. I was in the first plane with Jacques de Guelis, Edward (Teddy)
Bisset, an arms expert, and Andre Simon, a landing field expert—I
was the radio! I had done my wireless training at Henley-on-Thames
and had done 3 parachute jumps, one from a silent hot-air balloon,
quite frightening. The second plane carried the second commander
Thomas, a desperately needed surgeon, Ian Mackenzie, Jean Lannon a
second wireless operator. Of all the group I had only met Bisset before
and knew him well. I had no idea of our destination in France where
we were to be dropped—sitting next to him on the flight he told me
we'd be jumping in "near Limoges." I knew if I needed an escape route
it would be by the eastern Pyrenees. I had silk maps folded into my
epaulettes and chose not to accept a cyanide tablet.

It was chilly on the flight but it passed pretty quickly though I don't
remember being frightened at the prospect of dropping into occupied
Europe. Perhaps the very generous supper provided at Harrington
prevented any sinking feeling. I did run thru in my mind my parachute

drills. I really felt relieved and excited that I was now about to join in the fight for freeing France. This was a month after D-day and heavy fighting in Normandy. My turn came and obeying the dispatcher I was through the hole drifting down to moonlight. I did see trees but landed safely in a field. Later I knew this field was the "Clos de Sussac" about 3 miles from the village of Sussac. My landing was perfect—in no time I was free of my parachute and being helped by a reception committee member. We went by truck into the village and were taken to a building in the little village square, ushered into a back room and it was here I met Jean Claude Guiet, the radio for Salesman II. He had been in France for a long deadly month already. I remember having a drink with him followed by a hearty supper including a suckling pig! I was surprised I was so hungry. After the meal Jean Claude took me to a house around the corner and I fell into a very comfortable bed exhausted after a momentous and unforgetta-ble day. In the morning I walked into the village square enjoying the heat of summer sun on my back. The others had gathered in the square and photos were taken, everyone was relaxed and casual. We had 2 or 3 days in Sussac during which I got in touch with London informing them that we had gotten in safely. We moved off to the south escorted by Jean Claude, Liewer and local Resistance escorting us through heavily enemy-patrolled countryside. We ended up at Chadebec where I began my Tilleul transmissions.

I met with Jean Claude, again at the Prix d'Armes Ceremony in Limoges in September where Col. Rivier decorated the Missions.

Since escorting our Tilleul mission to Chadebec, Jean Claude had participated in four weeks of heavy running battles thru mid and late July, including the battle of Châteauroux and Mt Gargan.

Beating the long odds, Jean Claude had been in occupied France for more than fifteen weeks as we wound up and closed down the missions.

After a brief leave I ended my war in Burma and Sumatra in 1946.

MEDALS, RIBBONS, AND DISTINCTIONS

JEAN CLAUDE GUIET

UNITED STATES

Silver Star Medal

World War II Victory Medal European Theater

World War II Europe–Africa–Middle East Campaign Medal
(1941–1945) (with two Bronze Stars)

Asiatic Pacific Campaign Medal—World War II Ribbon (with one
Bronze Star)

Parachutist Badge with Combat Star

Congressional Gold Medal

FRANCE

Croix de Guerre French Government (Bronze Star)

Croix de Guerre French Resistance Guingouin (Bronze Star)

French Medal of the Resistance

PHILIPPE LIEWER

UNITED KINGDOM
Military Cross

FRANCE
Croix de Guerre Bronze Palm (with two Bronze Stars)

VIOLETTE SZABO

UNITED KINGDOM
George Cross
France and Germany Star
1939–1945 Star
1939–1945 War Medal

FRANCE
Croix de Guerre (with one Bronze Star)
French Medal of the Resistance

BOB MALOUBIER

FRANCE
Knight of the Legion of Honour
1939–1945 War Cross with three citations (with one Bronze Palm
     and two Stars)
Chevalier Medal of the French Resistance
Medal of Escapees
Colonial Medal Button "Far East"

Medal of Free France
1939–1945 War Commemorative Medal (with four clasps)
Insignia of the wounded soldiers

UNITED KINGDOM

Most Excellent Order of the British Empire (MBE)
Distinguished Service Order (DSO)
Order of the British Empire (OBE) (2014)
1939–45 Star
France and Germany Star

LAOS

Commander of the Royal Order of the Million Elephants

The tin bread box, container of Jean Claude's secrets.

ACKNOWLEDGMENTS

For my father's seventieth birthday I gave him a laptop computer. It was March 15, 1994. Growing up I had sensed that our family life was unusual, but I didn't understand how or why. I asked my father to write his life story—just for the children, and especially the grandchildren. He resisted, claiming that his personal history was ordinary and wouldn't interest anyone.

But he began to write, and before long he was so absorbed that my mother grew frustrated with his focus on "that damned machine." When we visited he would give me a stack of three-and-a-half-inch diskettes for safekeeping, with instructions not to open the files until after his death. Dad had the usual septuagenarian's issues operating his laptop, and, leaning over his shoulder to show him one function or another, I began to get glimpses of what he was setting down—not his autobiography, but an account of his secret war.

When he was done he gave my sister and me paper copies of his manuscript. About the same time, in the late 1990s, some of the official files pertaining to his service began to be declassified. In 1999 I received a phone call from England from a person looking for Mr. Guiet. I asked what the call was about, and was told that a museum would be opening to honor the memory of a secret agent my father had served with—Violette Szabo, a name I had learned just recently from the manuscript. My wife, Carol, and I took Dad to the museum opening, where he was reunited with Bob Maloubier. Dad also had an intensely moving meeting with Leo Marks, SOE's codemaster. The two men had known each other well—Marks had been on the receiving end of many of my father's coded transmissions, learning his "fist"— but until then they had never met face-to-face.

A year later we took my father back to the site of his wartime mission, the Haute-Vienne region in France. Dad told stories, I took notes. In Sussac a man on a bicycle figured out what we were doing and invited us to follow him to the home of a woman who had been active in the Resistance. She remembered a young American radio operator, and after asking Dad a lengthy series of careful questions she decided that yes, this must be him. Phone calls were made, and meetings were quickly scheduled with other veterans of the Resistance, who told more stories. For their contributions to this book, I am grateful.

Together with my coauthor, Tim Smith, I would also like to express thanks to our dear mutual friends, Claudine and Roger Parloff, who introduced us to one another and sparked this collaboration. We are also grateful for the assistance of David and Carole Harrison, who provided copies of original SOE documents; to Rosemary Rigby MBE, founder of the Violette Szabo Museum; and to Ken Rendell and Paul Cook at the International Museum of World War II, which is now the repository of Jean Claude Guiet's original OSS and SOE documents, photographs, and memorabilia. It has been an honor, while researching this book, to make the acquaintance of James Edgar, my father's old comrade in arms, and his wife, Valerie.

Our thanks are due also to Scott Moyers, our editor at Penguin Press; to his eagle-eyed associate, Mia Council; and to our perspicacious agent, Kris Dahl at ICM.

On a personal note, I, Dan, would like to thank my sons, Peter and

Eric Sakadinsky for their decades of support, help, and patience, on behalf of this story; Olivia Sakadinsky for her excellence in editing and research assistance; and most of all my wife, Carol, who undertook this endeavor and shared in its lengthy journey of discovery, and without whom this book would never have been completed.

And I, Tim, would like to thank my wife, Jennifer, who fills my days with sunshine.

NOTES

FOREWORD

1. M. R. D. Foot, *SOE in France* (London: Frank Cass, 2004), 236

CHAPTER I

1. M. R. D. Foot, *SOE in France* (London: Frank Cass, 1966), 60.

CHAPTER 2

1. M. R. D. Foote, *SOE in France*, ix.
2. Mark Seaman, *Special Operations Executive: A New Instrument of War* (Abingdon, Oxfordshire, UK: Routledge, 2006), 19.
3. A. R. B. Linderman, *Rediscovering Irregular Warfare: Colin Gubbins and the Origins of Britain's Special Operations Executive* (Norman, Okla.: University of Oklahoma Press, 2016), 166.
4. M. R. D. Foot, introduction to *The Secret History of S.O.E.*, by William Mackenzie (London: Saint Ermin's, 2002), xix.
5. Foot, introduction to *The Secret History of S.O.E.*, xx.

CHAPTER 3

1. M. R. D. Foot, *SOE in France* (London: Frank Cass, 1966), 44.
2. Philip Liewer SOE personal file; Crown copyright September 1942, National Archives, U.K.
3. Susan Ottaway, *Violette Szabo: The Life That I Have* (London: Thistle, 2014), 358–62.
4. R. J. Minney, *Carve Her Name with Pride* (London: George Newnes, 1956), 262–64.
5. Selwyn Jepson, Imperial War Museum, London, Oral History catalogue number 9331, reel 1, 1986.

6. Minney, *Carve Her Name with Pride,* chapter 8.
7. Bob Maloubier, *Agent Secret de Churchill* (Paris: Tallandier, 2011), 59.

CHAPTER 4

1. An account of this action, taken from Philippe's report to SOE, is cited in Foot's *SOE in France.* Additional detail is recorded in Maloubier's autobiography, *Agent Secret de Churchill.*

CHAPTER 5

1. Leo Marks, *Between Silk and Cyanide* (New York: HarperCollins, 1998), 11.
2. Marks, *Between Silk and Cyanide,* 198.
3. Susan Ottaway, *Violette Szabo: The Life That I Have* (London: Thistle, 2014), 132.

CHAPTER 7

1. Douglas Waller, *Wild Bill Donovan: The Spymaster Who Created the OSS and Modern American Espionage* (New York: Free Press, 2011), 51.
2. Waller, *Wild Bill Donovan,* 74.
3. John Whiteclay Chambers II, *Office of Strategic Services Training During World War II* (Washington, D.C., Studies in Intelligence, vol. 54, no. 2, Central Intelligence Agency, June 2010), 9.

CHAPTER 8

1. John Whiteclay Chambers II, *Bang-Bang Boys, Jedburghs, and the House of Horrors: A History of OSS Training and Operations in World War II* (Washington, D.C.: National Park Service, 2008), 192.
2. Bradley F. Smith and Agnes F. Petersen (eds.), *Heinrich Himmler: Geheimreden 1933 bis 1945 und andere Ansprachen* (Berlin: Ullstein, 1974), 169.

CHAPTER 10

1. M. R. D. Foot, *SOE in France* (London: Frank Cass, 1966), 79
2. The year 1944 was a leap year.

CHAPTER 11

1. For an excellent explanation of the double transposition system, and of all the others used by SOE, see Pierre Lorain, *Clandestine Operations: The Arms and Techniques of the Resistance, 1941–1944* (New York: Macmillan, 1972).

CHAPTER 14

1. Gordon Thomas and Greg Lewis, *Shadow Warriors of World War II: The Daring Women of the OSS and SOE* (Chicago: Chicago Review Press, 2017), 61–62.

CHAPTER 16

1. Max Hastings, *Das Reich: The March of the 2nd SS Panzer Division Through France, June 1944* (London: Michael Joseph, 1981), 113.

CHAPTER 30

1. R. J. Minney, *Carve Her Name with Pride* (London: George Newnes, 1956), 262–64.
2. Yeo-Thomas letter to Lieutenant Colonel Leonard Henry ("Dizzy") Dismore, September 14, 1944, Crown copyright 1944, National Archives, U.K.

CHAPTER 31

1. André Malraux, *Discours du transfert des cendres de Jean Moulin au Panthéon* (Paris, National Archives, Ministry of Culture, 1964).

INDEX

Page numbers in *italics* refer to illustrations.